It Just Happened The Other Day

— A TRUE STORY —

By Jonas Cain

Published by Positivity Magic Publishing
Boston, MA

ISBN-13: 978-1507829554
ISBN-10: 1507829558

First Edition ©January 2010
Seventh Edition ©January 2018

For more information visit
www.PositivityMagic.com

ABOUT THE AUTHOR

Jonas Cain is a positivity expert, author, comedy magician, and facilitator of fascination. For over two decades he's worked to engage, empower, and encourage individuals, corporations, and organizations to become Positivity Leaders that excel in their work, in their homes, and in their lives.

Through his engaging keynote presentations, interactive corporate workshops, motivational magic performances, and empowering mentoring sessions, Jonas has worked with major corporations, organizations, universities, sporting teams, military installations, and countless individuals, sharing research, tools, and strategies for developing and fostering positivity in all areas of life.

For more information on his programs, or if you'd like to invite Jonas to speak with your group, visit:

www.JonasCain.com

READER REVIEWS OF JONAS CAIN'S BOOKS

Great Love & True Emotion!!

"From the first page, I was hooked. The author expressed such great love and true emotion. A tender and tragic story. Thank you for sharing your heart!"

Cari S. / Amazon.com Reviewer

★★★★★

Truly Inspirational!

"Incredibly empowered by this book. His spirit and love of life is truly inspirational. Highly recommend this book to anyone. Great short read!"

Heather Neal / Amazon.com Reviewer

★★★★★

Rediscovery of How to Live!

"This book contains all the required principles for living a happy life. It draws from a variety of excellent sources to instruct the reader in achieving their goals. I highly recommend you read and ponder it as a fine wine being tasted and enjoyed for the first time."

Vulcanicus / Amazon.com Reviewer

★★★★★

Amazing!

"Probably the best book I ever read in a long time, for the stories, the horror, the laughs, the tears, and for the slaps to the heads. This is a book every human on this earth should read and experience what it is like to live."

Jeff P. / Amazon.com Reviewer

★★★★★

The Right Information!

"We all have tough times and everyone handles it differently. Jonas chose to use his experience to help others. This book came to me at an opportune moment. I just finished Making Things Happen, by Cathy Sticker, and this book picked up where I was left. Nicely done, Jonas. Keep up the good work!"

Julie / Amazon.com Reviewer

★★★★★

A LIFE-Changing Book!

"It Just Happened the Other Day is an 'I can't put it down book and let me read it again!!!' It has life, love, joy, sadness, beginning and endings—truly a book for young and old. It is a book that has to touch one's heart and open one's life to what "love" is truly about! It is an easy read but has great depth!! A great gift for anyone!!! The best gift to yourself. It is life changing!!"

Leah / Amazon.com Reviewer

★★★★★

He Does Everything With Passion!

"The story he shared was a very personal one. It was inspirational. He exposed something he experienced in his life to show his readers that even when you face the darkest times that there is always a reason to forge ahead. I could connect with his words and it was well worth every page. Jonas is an incredible writer, magician and overall just a great person. Everything he does he does with passion and you will not be disappointed if you decide to read his book or attend one of his shows."

Liane Muise

★★★★★

For You

CONTENTS

INTRODUCTION

With the gift of time I've discovered that pain eventually gives way to new joys and new pains and new amazing things to be fascinated by. The story in this book shares a small part of what played a big role in this Journey of Discovery. I'm excited to see what's next!

Jonas Cain
January 2018

"It seems life is a puzzle. When oddly shaped pieces present themselves, you may wonder how they could ever fit into your life—but then one day something happens and all of a sudden those seemingly out-of-place pieces find a perfect fit in your life revealing a beautiful picture—a picture that is you."

CHAPTER 1
— As Above —
April 2, 2008

*L*eft my apartment early with plenty of time to make the train to take my blues away. Walked slowly, reflecting on where I was going, where I had been and where I found myself. The sky was clear, lightly salted with a starry starry night. For the first time in a long long time I thought to myself, *"I'm going to miss being alive."*

Dark and alone, I arrived at the crossing with plenty of time to spare. I talked to myself. I talked to God. I talked to a tree. I felt vibrations below my feet and heard the train coming, riding down the bend. The red warning lights began to flash as the whistle blew louder. I turned away from the approaching light and stared down the dark track that lay ahead of me. The vibrations grew stronger as I closed my eyes. "Here I come."

But then there were running footsteps heading toward me. Opened my eyes just in time to see a familiar figure push me off track just as the train went crashing by. Trying to stand on my own, I wrestled with the man above me only to discover that there was no one above. It was only me.

CHAPTER 2
— An Introduction—

As a teenager, around the age of fifteen or so, I dreamed of going on a bicycle ride. Not merely a ride around town; no, not even just a day trip. But a journey! Lasting days, weeks, months, years! Don't know what it was that inspired such an ambition. I was riding my bicycle a lot during that time as I was not yet old enough to have a driver's license, yet old enough to not want to be home anymore. I always had bigger plans. Perhaps the bicycle represented my ticket to freedom; a freedom from where I was, who I had been and to where and who I was meant to become.

We never truly know why we imagine such things until the day that a few key pieces of the puzzle fill in the space between dream and reality, revealing a beautiful picture; a picture that's always been there yet not yet ready to be seen.

I spent the early years of my childhood growing up in a small Western Massachusetts town. Warren is an interesting town, with a D.A.R.E. Officer addicted to drugs, a resident possessed by the devil and a trailer park built on a former leper colony. It was there that I spent the first ten years of my life.

Early on I had once heard that children should be seen not heard, and I took it to heart. Life was a serious matter, which made it impossible for me to find humor in anything. And I'd often ask my parents if I could wear my Sunday clothes even just to play around the house. One Halloween my parents threw a costume party for me and my school friends, but I could not enjoy myself. The children were being children, loudly enjoying themselves. I hid away in my bedroom until my mother told me that parties are supposed to be loud. I guess not everyone had heard the "seen but not heard" rule.

Was incredibly organized, always with something to clean and tidy up. One day my mother had to punish me for cleaning my room too much. *"Stop cleaning your room right this instant and watch TV!"* she yelled. I was devastated.

Even though I was a strict observer of the rules I secretly longed for something more. I found that children were too often told, *"You can't do this, you can't do that, sit down, shut up,"* yet in my mind all things were possible. Like the time I saw David Copperfield flying in the air. I can still remember sitting on the floor of my aunt's house watching the television, awestruck. If a grown man can do what no one is supposed to be able to do, then maybe there is something more?

For as long as I can remember I was always singing, making up songs and creating music with anything I found around me. One day I asked my folks if they would buy me a saxophone. At the time the instrument was bigger than I was so naturally they said no. That, and my family was of very modest means so they were reluctant to make such an expensive investment. It was the biggest thrill of my life the day they surprised me with a saxophone. Seventeen years later I can till remember not having a clue how to play a single note yet sitting alone in my bedroom making noise on the Jupiter alto saxophone anyway.

It wasn't until just after my eleventh birthday in 1994 when my family moved to the nearby town of Palmer that I started writing. The move was traumatic. I had been taken away from all that I had ever known. Just when I thought I knew something of life it was shown that nothing is ever for certain. That was the first time I lost my bearing on reality. Writing was my way of coping with that truth: the mystery of the unknown.

My passion for magic augmented that same year. It has been said that we must embrace what we most fear. It must have been human instinct that brought me to embrace the mystery that magic provided. Encouraged by my father, he brought me every week to *Bianco's Bike and Magic Shop* in Feeding Hills to meet and learn from the local masters of magic...and buy and repair bicycles (an odd combination, I know). Perhaps my greatest magic trick of all was performed just two years after moving to Palmer when I returned to my hometown to perform my first public magic show. The shy kid who hardly spoke a word was now in front of the entire third grade class of *Warren Community Elementary School* performing the impossible. Overcoming shyness, finally expressing the inner dreams of a magical world to an audience of fellow children; indeed, boldly stepping forward and performing regardless of my introversion was perhaps my first real magic trick.

My readings became bizarre. *Man Myth and Magic: the illustrated Encyclopedia of the Supernatural* and *The Enchanted World of Wizards and Witches* were two of my favorite books at the time. The magic I had been learning were simple tricks, puzzles disguised as magic; but I wanted the real thing. My writings took on deeper subjects. Frustrated that I was not able to find the answers to the mysteries that I was looking for I decided to create my own mystery artificially in a theatre production; a magical play that combined magic with music and poetry. This theatre production, I imagined, would perhaps quench my thirst to express this magical world I saw in my mind's eye. Pages and pages were

5

written in my notebooks, filled with ideas and descriptions of the stage set and themes for this production. Then high school happened.

It is perhaps human nature that once we realize that we want something we want it yesterday. From an early age I knew what I wanted to do, but school was getting in the way of that. Time was not moving fast enough so one spring day in 1998 I came home from school and put my father's shotgun to my head and pulled the trigger.

Click

Wasn't loaded

As calm as I appeared on the outside, on the inside I was an anxious wreck. There were no bullets to save me from waiting so waiting was just what I had to do. Then I fell in love.

CHAPTER 3
— A Greater Meaning —
August 5, 2007

*I*t was a typical Sunday evening at LaNotte
Restaurante in East Windsor, CT. The place was
empty save a few people at the bar and a table of
two nearby. It was an older couple, maybe
around the age of sixty or seventy years old. It
struck me that the gentleman looked a lot like
Elvis, complete with big jet-black, slicked hair and
glasses. I imagined it to be what Elvis would have
looked like had he moved to Connecticut instead
of dying. I approached the couple with my
standard pick-up line and a smile and shared my
magic with them.

What magic I performed for them is not
important for this story. What is important is that
we had some laughs and some smiles and then it
was off to the table with the family that had just
arrived in the dining room where I again used my
pick-up line with a smile and shared my magic
with them. After leaving that table my attention
was drawn to the group of people that had formed
around the older couple. There was a huge
commotion and it became apparent that the
woman had choked on a piece of food. She was
ok, though the EMTs were called as a precaution.

9

When the EMTs left and the whole ordeal was over the woman was visibly distraught. Too distraught for such a minor occurrence.

I walked over to the table to try and comfort the woman. Her makeup got all over my pin stripped suit. She needed the hug so I didn't mind. She was crying as she told me her story:

A month earlier she was at this very same restaurant and sitting at the very same table, and on that day she also choked. But on that day she nearly died. She could not cough up the piece of food. A man sitting at the bar went to her to perform the Heimlich maneuver but it wasn't working. For what must have seemed an eternity for her she turned grey as the air was kept form her lungs. The man just kept pounding and pounding on the frail woman as she was on her way out of this life. Finally, just moments before it would have been too late the food was at last dislodged from her esophagus. It was then that the EMTs finally arrived and upon hearing how the Good Samaritan had pounded so hard on her for so long they feared that he may have broken her ribs and so she was transported to the hospital. They did not find any broken ribs but what they did find was an aneurism that was about to burst. Had this near-death experience not happened this woman surely would have died.

The rest of my night at work was a blur after hearing her story, and on the ride home all I could think of is how choking had saved her life. It reminded me of all my problems, big and small. I thought that maybe they were saving my life too.

CHAPTER 4
— A Dream —

*H*ad a dream last night that I was having lunch with my Grandmother. We were talking quietly for a while before I finally said, "I thought you died, how is it that I am having lunch with you?"

"I didn't really die," she replied.

"But we buried you?" I said.

"That wasn't really me."

"Where did you go then?"

"I went somewhere else for a while."

Then I woke up.

CHAPTER 5
— The Dance —
December 3, 1999

We danced the night away. Although I was only sixteen I knew that with what little I knew of love I was in love with Stephanie. There was just something about her. The way she sang, discovering songs in the moment. The way she played like she was a child even though she was two years older than me. The way she smiled; the way she made me feel. The way we were able to look into each other's eyes, as if our souls were talking to each other.

It was a big deal that I asked Stephanie to go to the Winter Formal with me. I had never asked a girl out before, never even asked for a dance before. But Stephanie was different. She was an exception. She was exceptional. There we were at the dance, dancing the night away. We sat for a moment against the wall in the decorated cafeteria of the high school. Just then a slow song came on. I desperately wanted to dance with Stephanie but I couldn't bring myself to ask her; even though she was *my* date! We had danced to every other song but I couldn't muster the nerve to ask Stephanie to dance with me.

"Who am I?" I thought, *"This is Stephanie sitting next to me! Who am I to ask* her *to dance?"* Meanwhile she just sat there waiting for me to ask.

Then another guy walked up to Stephanie and asked her to dance.

"Who does this guy think he is!?!" I thought to myself. Of course she said yes.

There I sat watching everyone else dancing; the world on my mind. As the song ended Stephanie walked up to me and said the words that would stick with me for the rest of my life.

"You know Jonas, if you want to dance with me all you have to do is ask."

Then she walked away.

CHAPTER 6
— The Song —
Spring 2000

We were lost. Stephanie spotted a police officer and thought it would be a good idea to ask him for directions, and to get his attention she drove her car up onto the sidewalk.

Stephanie and I had been spending a lot of time together and one of my favorite things was going on adventures in her car. Those rides always seemed to lead to something bad happening with her car. Whether it be driving through a red light at an intersection because her car lost all power and could not stop, or having to use stolen duct tape to patch up hoses under the hood, or being pulled over by the police for driving on the sidewalk; being with Stephanie truly was an adventure and I loved every minute of it.

"Should I get out of the car?" Stephanie asked me.

"No! Stay in the car Stephanie!" I strongly recommended, not wanted her to get into any more trouble than she was already in. But I had nothing to be concerned about. In a way that only Stephanie can, she explained to the officer her reason for driving on the sidewalk and he was happy to give directions. I don't know how she does it. There is just something about her.

I was thinking about all of our adventures together one day while at school. I had my saxophone out and I was just playing around. It was the afternoon and most everyone else had left for the day so I was all alone in the band room, but I wanted to be with Stephanie. Closed my eyes and started to play. I played *It's in Every One of Us* by David Pomeranz; one of my most favorite songs as it embodies all that Stephanie is. A simple, beautiful melody. I imagined that Stephanie was there with me, listening to me playing for her. I imagined our eyes meeting, looking into each other's souls. And when I opened my eyes...there she was! Stephanie! Standing in the doorway listening to my music! It was the best magic trick I had ever performed. I never told her that I was playing it for her, but I knew she knew. She always knew that I loved her; I didn't have to tell her. But I did anyway.

> *"It's in every one of us to be wise.*
> *Find your heart; open up both your eyes.*
> *We can all know everything,*
> *without ever knowing why.*
> *It's in every one of us, by and by."*

CHAPTER 7
— Journal Entry —
September 30, 2008

I have this theory that the meaning of life is death. For from the moment that we are born we begin the process of dying; for to age (grow up; grow old) is to begin to decay. The problem with this notion is that it makes waking up each day and being a productive part of society difficult. For if the meaning of life is to die then everything else that we could possibly do is meaningless. Better to get busy dying, for it is only in death that we can truly live. For to live is to die, and to die is to live. With this perspective one finds no point in doing anything at all and becomes content in doing nothing at all. Do you see my dilemma? Each morning I wake up with this idea and each day I convince myself that I'm wrong, that there is a point to all this other than death. But when night comes I'm right back to where I started, wanting nothing more than death. I went to a high school football game today and it occurred to me that if 'move' is pronounced 'moove' then why isn't 'love' pronounced 'loove'? Does any of this make sense? These are the things that keep me up at night.

CHAPTER 8
— The Park bench —
August 3, 2007

"**B**ut I'll miss you!"

Stephanie and I were on a walk around her neighborhood when I told her I was planning to move to Texas for business. I had never been there but I got a tip that Texas was the place to be for entertainment.

Just the day earlier I was on my way home from a gig when I got a call on my cell from Stephanie. She asked me what I was doing the next day and I told her I wasn't doing anything after work, and asked what she was doing. "Hanging out with you," she said. Stephanie always knew how to get exactly what she wanted.

I didn't understand what the problem was with me moving to Texas. "I'll only be a phone call away," I explained.

"But you'll be so far away and I'll miss you," she pouted.

I still didn't get it. For years Stephanie had rejected me. Right from the very beginning I told Stephanie that I was head over heels in love with her but she always remained adamant that we were just friends and would never be anything more than that. That was always fine with me. I just wanted to be around her. As long as we stayed in each other's lives I was ok. I just wanted to be there for her.

A year earlier in 2006 I had gone to New York City to audition for the first season of *America's Got Talent*. I traveled all morning before getting into a line that wrapped around the building, and the block, and the next block. There were so many people there, too many people in fact. They gave half the line passes to go back the next day. I held the pass in my hand looking at it knowingly. Knowing that it is the single most important opportunity of my career and also knowing that I couldn't go back the next day. I had something far more important to do. I had promised Stephanie that I would drive her to the airport. Anyone could drive her to the airport, but I wanted to do it. I wanted to be there for her. I didn't tell her about the audition; she wouldn't have liked that I was blowing it off to help her out. She would have refused my help and told me to go to New York. She always loved my magic.

We walked a little more in silence. I was still trying to understand why Stephanie was so upset about my plans to move when she finally said, "Ok, how about this: if by the time we're forty, if we don't find anyone else, let's get married."

"I love that idea! Let's do it!" I said.

After a silent pause she asked, "Would you marry me just because?"

"No," I replied, "I would marry you because you are the love of my life."

As the evening turned to night we arrived at the park bench in the park across the street from her home. There was a summer storm rumbling in the distance. The air was purple. We looked into each other's souls.

"Would we work?" she asked.

"I don't know," I said. "We've never given it a chance."

What we had been avoiding for eight years was now staring us in the face. What seemed so complicated for oh so long all of a sudden appeared to be oh so easy. We held each other close. Our eyes were so close that it was all we could see and our hearts raced faster than they've ever raced before. She was waiting for me to do what I knew she wanted me to do. It reminded me of that night at the dance and I didn't want to wait too long and lose my chance again.

Yet I hesitated. I was scared. What I had been pursuing for eight years was finally staring me in the face. In that moment I realized that the success of happiness comes with a great responsibility. Was I ready for that responsibility?

"This is such a beautiful moment," Stephanie said softly, "I never want it to end." She paused for me to act. Or for me to say something or do anything. All I could do was stare into her eyes. It was like I was looking into my destiny and instinctly knew the repercussions of the events of this night for years to come and it was as if she too knew the true meaning of what we were doing even though neither of us could see the storm that lay ahead. After another moment she added, "But then the moment passes." This was my chance. As it turns out, my last chance. If I didn't act now my hopes of ever being with Stephanie would be lost forever. For years I had rewired my brain. Stephanie was just my best friend. A very special best friend. She waited a moment longer then finally said the word that pushed me into action. "Chicken." With hearts racing our lips danced and my world was turned inside out. In that moment I knew what it was to die happy for in that moment I actually felt like we had died and our souls were living out our one last wish before leaving the physical world.

"I think I've ruined you for every other woman," Stephanie said.

"There's no one else for me," I said. "It has always been you."

I no longer feared death for I had everything I ever wanted. Why should I be so lucky? Death, it seemed, would be the logical next step.

CHAPTER 9
— Journal Entry —
December 5, 2007

I don't know what I was expecting last night as I lay in bed still wearing my suit. I guess it was my way of being prepared in case it was my turn to go. These anniversaries seem to happen every day now. Wasn't even tired yet. My sleep has been disturbing lately, whether it happens or not. As I awoke this morning I couldn't get my mind off what happened three months ago today, and how it may have went down. The air in my apartment is cold; we're conserving oil for the lack of money and as a consequence I curse the air every day. So I stayed incubated under the blanket in bed for hours recalling the events of September 5th.

Last night as I laid there holding the picture of us it occurred to me that maybe what happened really didn't happen. How could it have? How absurd for such an event to occur! How could it be? I feel asleep for a little while before finally repositioning myself to put head to pillow and turned off the light. I then pretended that December 4 was actually September 4, and I turned my light back on to look at the picture of us, just as I had done that night three months earlier. What happened really did happen. But maybe now it's my turn? The morning came and proved otherwise. The same question that crossed my mind back in August came back to me, *"Why should I be so lucky?"* Only this time I was asking for a different reason and I really didn't consider myself to be all that lucky. It's all a matter of perspective I suppose. Just in case today really was September 5th I called Stephanie at 7:01AM to talk to her on her way to work. Once again she didn't answer her phone, only this time I couldn't leave a message. How am I supposed to do this? How do people do this? This is the most absurd thing I have ever experienced. And when I say absurd what I mean by that is f#@%ed up. This whole thing is messing with me. What am I supposed to do? I don't really want to do anything but I know I have to do something. What does that leave me with? In the Chinese Zodiac 2007 is the year of the Pig and having been born in 1983 I am a pig. 2007, the year of Jonas. And so this is Christmas, what have I done? I have done a lot this year, including accomplishing my biggest, most wildest dream. And yet I have nothing to show for it; only memories. People tell me to keep those memories but to also move on from them. I can't do that. Why would I want to? And even if I did want to, how could I? It would be like free falling through the air. At first it feels wonderful, almost like you're flying. Then all of a sudden you hit the ground and your body is mangled beyond unrecognition. Do people really expect you to get up and walk away from a fall like that? To move on from that, like everything is fine, would truly be a miracle. I would rather stay on the ground dreaming that I'm still flying, because my broken dreams are all that I'm left with anyway.

Three down. How many more to come? I don't even want to think about it. For while it seems impossible that three months have already gone by, yet it also feels like an eternity. Perhaps I was right when I said that life is too short and too long all at the same time. For now all I know is that I'm still stuck wearing this black and blue suit, the physical representation of what's going on inside of me; just like my actual body is the physical representation of my soul. I'm looking forward to meeting myself someday. I wonder what it'll be like. I'll have a lot of questions to ask. I wonder if my soul wears me to bed at night.

CHAPTER 10
— Car Broke Down —
January 2008

Got in the car Thursday night and started her up. I was leaving right on time to get to my gig in Enfield, CT. It was to be a quick in and out engagement at a cocktail party at the corporate office of a big financial company. As I pulled out of my driveway the car felt "funny" as I drove down the street. I knew something was up but I was "right on time" for leaving so there was no way I was going to stop and check it out (not the best way to deal with problems but it's one way to live). As I merged onto the Mass Pike the car started to shake a bit. "Just get me to the gig," I said out loud before adding, "In time to do the show!" I smiled at my foresight to be specific with my request. I've often been told that God is a man, so when we pray we have to be specific. Otherwise we'll get what we wanted just not *exactly* what we had in mind. So I drove the half-hour to Enfield, got off the highway and turned right onto the street that the venue was on. That's when the crunching, cranking and other awful noises started up. The car coasted to the front of the building that the gig was in and wouldn't go any further. I was amazed at my luck; the car broke down exactly where I asked it to! Left the car there to deal with it after the performance.

The show went well as always and afterwards I rode in the tow truck to drop my car off at the mechanic. On our way there I called my roommate Jason to give me a ride back to the apartment and that is where this story takes an interesting turn. You see, just the night before this all happened I was on my way home from a gig and I suddenly had the urge to go to the local bar. Been getting that urge a lot lately but I usually fight it and go straight home. Not so that night. I had some drinks and some laughs with the locals and even won $100 on Keno; a nice way to end the night! Yet there we were, the very next night, on our way home and Jason decided it would be a good idea to stop at the bar; the very same bar that I was at just the night before. We had some drinks and a few laughs and I again won $100 on Keno! What are the odds of that? $200 in two days? It's not every day something like that happens, and that is the purpose of this story. The next day I picked up the car from the mechanic and he gave me the repair bill. It came to exactly $200. One may say that the car breaking down robbed me out of the luck I had received with the $200, but I prefer to see it from the other side of the coin. I like to see it as a gift from the Universe giving me exactly what I needed when I needed it. Such a belief would prove that we already have all that we need, and whatever we may need along the way will be supplied to us in abundance. If given the choice, I choose to believe in that perspective.

CHAPTER 11
— Journal Entry —
January 3, 2008

Where does all this time go? There is so much of it, yet it doesn't even exist, but for not existing it is running way too fast! Where does it all go? It's almost been four months. Four months! How? How could four months have gone by? Everything moves on, and nothing is ever the same, but for the past four months everything has been the same. Nothing has moved on except time. Time is marching forward, why can't I? How could I anyway? I'm still stuck in four months ago. *Wake me up when September ends.* I'm still sleeping in September, dreaming of the wonderful things that happened right next to the awful thing that happened. The thoughts of the wonderful lifetime ahead of me! And then just twenty-four hours later how everything changed. And now my mind is forever restless with the thoughts not of the lifetime ahead of me, but now of the dark days ahead. *What a difference a day made.* Why can't I just *Let it Be?* Indeed, please do wake me up when September ends, but *when you're dreaming with a broken heart the waking up is the hardest part.* I feel like a balloon full of helium, but my string is tethered preventing me from soaring. Does any of this make sense?

CHAPTER 12
— Sleepless Night —
August 25 – 26, 2007

"I have something to show you," I told Stephanie, "follow me."

She was on another one of her "I'm no good for you" rants. She was always trying to protect me from her. We had spent the whole evening at a friend's house party but now it was late and most everyone had gone home or passed out on the living room floor. I led Stephanie out of the house and down the long porch steps to the car. I opened the passenger door and let her in then walked to the driver's side and got in. I picked up my sunglasses.

A few days earlier Stephanie had come over my apartment and we lay together in my bed looking into each other's eyes when she said, "I think I've already hurt you and you just don't know it yet." I didn't know how to answer a statement like that. She always warned me that loving her would bring only great pain. Maybe I was a fool for risking that pain to experience love. Maybe I'm the biggest fool I know. But that late night in my car I had an answer to let Stephanie know that despite her warnings I wasn't going anywhere.

"These are my favorite sunglasses," as I handed them to her. "I got them just last year and they became my favorite pair ever. There was just something about them." Stephanie examined them, perplexed. And rightfully so. They were in rough shape. I continued, "It didn't take long for the glasses to show their imperfections. They quickly scratched, got bent out of shape, lost one of the screws that holds the right arm on, and a nose guard has gone missing. But they still serve the purpose that they were made for, so just because they're not perfect I'm not going to just throw them aside for a new pair. They're still my favorite pair of sunglasses. I love everything about them; no other pair will do."

Stephanie sat quietly looking at the sunglasses for a moment, "But I'm not a pair of sunglasses."

A lifetime of people giving up on Stephanie made her this way. I was there to show her that I would never give up on her. "You're right," I said, "you're not sunglasses. And you're also right that you're not perfect; but just like my sunglasses I love everything about you anyway and I never want to let you go."

We went back inside to find a place to sleep. Found a spot on the couch where no one had yet claimed and we sat down with her head in my lap. I didn't sleep at all that night. All I did was watch the time on the clock roll by with Stephanie lying next to me. I think that even if I could have slept I would not have wanted to. I didn't want to miss a single moment of it.

I left before anyone woke up. I went outside and stood the porch to watch the sunrise. "How did I get here?" I wondered out loud. That is a question that over the next few months would often return to me. I went out to breakfast alone. I needed to be alone with my thoughts. I couldn't even eat. I should have been hungry; I hadn't eaten anything the whole night before and only drank a lot of funny tasting punch. I never drank before, aside from a toast of champagne at my brother's wedding. With both of my parents being alcoholics I just avoided it.

Sitting quietly at the table I said a prayer for Stephanie. "Dear God, please make Stephanie happy for the rest of her life." I began to cry. It surprised me because I hadn't cried in years. I took my untouched meal to go and went home to pack for the gig I had later that afternoon, grabbed my saxophone and left for Longmeadow where I had a quick recording session with *Opel*, a vaguely folkish alternative rock band I had been playing with. We were recording our first full length album *Strange Encounters*. After practice I drove to Wilbraham for a quick birthday party magic show for my mechanic's daughter. Just as I began the show my cell phone vibrated. I usually turn my phone off when I perform but I wanted to know if Stephanie called. Sure enough Stephanie's face appeared on the screen. I had taken a picture of her a few days earlier and set the photo to show up anytime she called. Out of impulse I nearly answered the call but then I thought it would be best if I just called her back later. The show was a blur; after seeing her face I could only think of Stephanie. That performance would be the last of its kind as I would never again perform that particular show. I couldn't, for in the coming days my life would never be the same.

On the way home from the show I called Stephanie, pulling my car over in front of a church on Main St. in Wilbraham just before Monson Rd. I knew if I drove over the mountain to Monson that my cell phone's signal would cut out and I didn't want that interrupting our conversation. We talked about the party from the night before. We talked about her. We talked about me. We talked about us. We talked about my sunglasses. And just when we were really getting into the conversation my cell phone battery died.

Blast!

I always charge my phone overnight but because I didn't make it home the night before I didn't get around to doing that. I raced down the street in my car to the gas station. No pay phone. My only option was to now race over the mountain back to my apartment to use the back-up cell phone. I was driving top speed up the mountain hoping there were no speed traps that afternoon. That's when I saw the lemonade stand. I have a very firm rule about lemonade stands. Always stop. No matter what is going on, always stop. So I screeched to a halt, turned around and pulled into the driveway. The two little girls were so excited.

"We saw you drive by and turn around," they said with a smile, "Thank you for stopping!"

"Well I am very thirsty; I had to stop! How's business today?"

"Good," they said together. "We've had six people come by already."

"That's great! What are you saving up for?"

"We're going to Disney World!"

I bought two cups of lemonade for ten dollars (hefty tip included) and performed the world famous bunny trick for the two young entrepreneurs. I never turn down an opportunity to share some magic. Then it was back on the road to complete my mission of calling Stephanie back.

I made it in record timing. I switched the SIM card to my backup phone, ran outside to my back porch and called her number. No answer. I called again. No answer. I left a message. Then I noticed that she had left six voice messages in the time it took me to get to the phone. They were all filled with messages of hate and loath for my cell phone. Aside from the battery losing power, T-Mobile's reception was terrible at my apartment and would always cut off our conversations.

I went the rest of the day anxious to speak with her again. It took several hours but my phone finally rang. It was Stephanie! She was about to have dinner with her family and I asked if I could come over afterwards. She suggested that we get ice cream. I thought that was a wonderful idea. I was up for anything so long as it involved being with her. I began preparing to go but could not decide what to wear. I consulted Jason. He was of no help as he really didn't care; he pretended to though. I put on some shorts, a t-shirt and a red button up short sleeved collared shirt and left it unbuttoned. Jason said it looked good. I was going in. On my way I listened to the radio. As I got onto 91 South off of 291 West I changed the station and just as I did one of my favorite songs came on, *Run Around* by Blues Traveler. I sang along for a while then grew silent; the words suddenly had so much meaning and I wondered whether I was living the song right now. *"Why you gotta give me a run around?*

It's a sure fire way to speed things up but all it does is slow me down." The night proved otherwise (though the coming years would reveal that it did slow me down) but the thought was still in the back of my head, *"Like a nervous magician waiting in the wings."* I arrived at Stephanie's and she decided that she wasn't in the mood for ice cream. I admitted that I was not concerned about the ice cream and so we decided to go for a drive with no particular destination, ultimately ending up parked in a dark secluded high school parking lot.

"I like your outfit," Stephanie said.

"Thank you," I said, then thinking to myself, *"Thank you Jason!"* We sat in silence for a moment before I asked her, "What are you thinking about?"

"I'm wondering when you're going to get the nerve to ask me to be your girlfriend."

She always had a way of getting exactly what she wanted. We talked a bit more. I had asked her to be my girlfriend eight years earlier but I was a day late and she said no. I had missed my chance. But if there's one thing that Stephanie taught me it was to take every opportunity. If you want something you have to go out there and get it; no room for passive people. My opportunity had come again; if I didn't act now my chance would be gone again.

"Stephanie," I said, "Will you be my girlfriend?"

"I don't think I'm ready to be your girlfriend yet."

Blast!

Was she toying with me!?! I was not going to give up without a fight. I did the only thing I could do. I recounted the time I took her to the high school dance so many years earlier.

"We danced the whole night away, Stephanie," I started. "But for some reason, even though you were my date, I could not muster the nerve to ask you to dance with me to this one slow song. We just sat there as the music played. You were waiting for me to ask but I did nothing! I just sat there! Then this other guy walked up to you and asked you to dance. I thought to myself, *'Who the hell does this guy think he is!?!'* And you two got up on the dance floor while I just sat there passively. When the music ended you came up to me and said, 'You know Jonas, if you want to dance with me all you have to do is ask.' Stephanie, I'm tired of passively watching life from the sidelines. When is it going to be our turn? When's it going to be our turn to be happy? You deserve to be happy. I know you're scared, I'm scared too! I'm petrified! I've wanted this for eight years but I'm scared that I won't be good enough for you. I'm scared that you may someday realize that I'm not as special as you think I am. I'm scared that I might not always be able to be there for you. I'm scared that I might someday hurt you and I never want to do that. But I refuse to let my fears get in the way of me doing what I truly want to do. I'm ready and willing to jump in head first. Stephanie, will you dance with me?"

I was speaking figuratively with that last line but Stephanie took me literally so we got out of my car and danced to the sounds of the night. I finally got what I had been looking for. Stephanie was in love with me. She finally admitted it. After all these years of pushing me away I finally proved to her that I wasn't going anywhere no matter what may happen. I had earned her love and trust.

"You're right," she said, "I do deserve to be happy," then gasped. "Did I really just say that out loud?"

"Yes you did," I said smiling.

She finally understood. And she meant it. And what a wonderful moment it was.

"All right, August twenty-sixth," she said to herself. I think she was already planning our anniversaries in her mind.

"You amaze me, Stephanie Erin," I said to her.

Then she replied, "You don't have to keep calling me by my full name, I'm your girlfriend now. You can call me sweety, honey, baby..."

"But it's such a beautiful name," I quickly replied.

"But what will you do when I'm Stephanie Toutant?"

"I'll probably still call you Stephanie Erin. You'll always be my Stephanie Erin."

Then we talked of Valentine's Day, of all things. She said that it was one of her favorite holidays. Didn't need a big hint; I already started planning something special for Stephanie even though Valentine's Day was still six months away.

"What religion are you?" she asked. We had rarely talked about faith so I was a bit surprised by her question.

"I don't really have a religion," I said. "They all seem to teach the same messages of Peace, Love and Joy. What religion are you?"

"Catholic," she answered."

"Then so am I."

"Will you go to church Sunday with my family?"

"Yes I will."

It was getting late and Stephanie was starting her first official day at her new job the next morning so I soon brought her home. When we got back to her place I walked her to the door. We said our "goodbyes", our "I love yous", and our "I'll miss yous." We couldn't get enough one last kisses. When our hands pulled apart our finger tips were the last to pull away but our eyes never pulled away as the porch door closed and we kissed through the glass. I stumbled backwards down the steps as Stephanie fumbled with the door to the house, our eyes never leaving as the door slowly closed. I stood outside for a moment not wanting to leave. I reached into my pocket and removed one of my business cards. On the back of it I wrote a simple message, *"I hope you have a <u>Great</u> first day at work! I love you!"* and stuck the note in her car door. I knew she was anxious about her first day; perhaps this would make her smile for a while in the morning.

Stopped at a gas station just off of the entrance ramp to the Mass Pike on 291. I filled up the gas tank and went inside to get a beverage for the ride home. The woman behind the counter looked tired. It was then that I realized that it was now early Monday morning and I had been up since early Saturday morning. Drove home thinking about Stephanie as I laid in bed still thinking of her. She's taken over my life again.

CHAPTER 13
— Journal Entry —
February 24, 2006

I don't think that I will ever marry, but if I did it would have to be with Stephanie. A very special person who I care for more than anyone else in the world and who makes my world feel like heaven. But she says that we will never be. Yet she also says that I need to be more aggressive. That if I want something then I have to be aggressive and go out and get it. She knows how I feel about her, is this her way of saying that if I want to be with her then I have to be more aggressive about my desire? She says that she doesn't want passive people in her life. She's telling me to be aggressive, is this her way of telling me that she wants to be with me? My mind and soul are constantly awake with her consuming every minute of thought. I can't wait to see her again and hold her in my arms. I don't want to sleep because then I can't think about her, but if I don't sleep then I can't dream about her. I just want to be with her.

CHAPTER 14
— The Proposal —
August 29, 2007

We laid in her bed, staring into each other's eyes. I asked her, "What are you thinking about?"

She answered softly, "I'm willing you to ask." I knew what she was alluding to.

"But Stephanie, I don't have a ring yet."

"I don't care about the ring," she said, "You better hurry up and ask."

"Will you marry me?"

She smiled the biggest most beautiful smile as she said "Yes."

My heart sang! Never in my life had I felt that happy! It didn't seem like things could get any better yet every moment with Stephanie was more wonderful than the last! "I've always wondered what that would feel like," I said.

"What?"

"To ask the love of my life to marry me, for her say yes and to have that woman be you."

It had been eight years since I fell in love with her and now just three days after that Sunday evening in my car we were ready to spend the rest of our lives together. Dreams do come true. Why should I be so lucky?

CHAPTER 15
— Lying In Goose Poo —
October 6, 2007

As I stared up at the tree and the sky, and talked with Stephanie, my thoughts turned to the goose poo that I was laying in. I sat up and looked at all of the geese. When I pulled into the cemetery that afternoon I had to slow down because there were so many of them. I even nearly ran over one! There were so many geese, it was impossible to not notice the goose that waddled too close to the car. It was then that a piece of the puzzle revealed itself.

When we see a goose, what do we see? Do we see just a goose? No. We see geese. They are always together, never apart from their gaggle of family and friends. Had that goose been alone I would not have been driving as slowly as I was and would not have seen the goose in time to stop. By staying together the goose was able to survive. We have all been put on this Earth together; if we have any hope of survival then we too must stick together with our gaggle of family, friends and the whole of humanity.

Stephanie always has something wonderful to share when I visit.

CHAPTER 16
— Labor Day Weekend —
August 31 – September 3, 2007

"*B*ut I'm sentimental."

Stephanie looked at me with her beautiful brown eyes when she said it. We were driving through New Hampshire on our way to Lake Winnipesauke at Weirs Beach in Laconia, NH. We had stopped at the Long Horn Steakhouse in Keene for what turned out to be our first official date together as a couple. When we sat down she looked at me from across the table and said, "You'll learn that I don't like sitting across from you; I want to be by your side." She always knew how to get exactly what she wanted; never afraid to ask. I moved to sit next to her. I wasn't even hungry; just being next to Stephanie was enough to keep me alive.

I ordered pineapple juice and Stephanie ordered an adult pineapple beverage that came with a souvenir glass that we could take home. It was a nice memento of our weekend together to cherish for years to come. All during dinner Stephanie eyed the dessert menu on the table. Right on cover was the picture of their strawberry cheesecake.

"That looks so good," she said.

"You want the cheesecake? We'll get the cheesecake," I said. But halfway through the meal Stephanie said she was full.

"You're not too full for the cheesecake are you?" I asked.

"Yes," she said, "I'm too full for the cheesecake."

"Whoa whoa whoa!" I said, "You've been eying that cheesecake this whole time; even if you only eat a few bites you have to get the cheesecake. Life is too short." Writing these words now I am brought back to that moment as if I never left it. I write these words now to let go.

We got the cheesecake. And it was good. We only had a few bites but it was worth it. Never pass up an opportunity; it may be your last chance. After dinner we continued our journey to vacation. We got about twenty-minutes down the road when Stephanie looked at me suddenly, "We forgot our souvenir glass!"

I looked at her then at the time. "It's just a glass," I said. My sentimental brown eyed girl looked at me with those eyes and a moment later I did a U turn and headed back to the restaurant. It did not really matter to me what time it was or what we were doing but my family had expected us to be at the lake already and the time was getting late. I put them out of my mind. Stephanie had my full attention. We turned out

46

of the restaurant parking lot for the second time but had to stop at the traffic light at the plaza's exit. I leaned over to Stephanie and passionately kissed her sweet, sweet lips. I so loved the opportunities red lights had been affording me with Stephanie around. May we all be so blessed with red lights throughout our lives.

"BEEEEEEEEP!!!!!"

The car behind us impatiently sounded their horn. Our lips unlocked as Stephanie looked behind us and I looked ahead and saw the green light. It was getting much later in the evening and another twenty minutes up the road we'd see no other cars. We simply rode together in the easy silence.

"It's so quiet," she said, "So peaceful. I've never experienced this before. There's a CD in my car that has a song about this. No one has ever given me this sense of peace before. You're the only one. In the easy silence it's ok when there's nothing more to say. I wish I had brought the CD with us so you could listen to it." A moment later she reached over and turned the on radio. I think she was half expecting the song to be on the radio right then. Being out "in the boondocks", as she put it, no stations were coming in. She tried several and was about to give up when suddenly the static cleared and a song came through. We just looked at each other and smiled.

Every couple has a song and even though we had only been together less than a week, Stephanie and I already had ours. It was almost too perfect to be true; but the song that came through the static, when no other songs would, was our song: *Live Like You Were Dying.* Even though we were both afraid of heights we had plans to go skydiving together. We truly were crazy, quite insane really. We just held hands, smiled and sang along as we drove in the night. *"Someday I hope you get the chance to live like you were dying."* As the song ended the static returned and we couldn't get any more music to come in. Stephanie turned off the radio. "It was fate," she said.

When we finally got to the cottage we were so tired that we went straight to bed. We laid in each other's arms, and once again I did not want to sleep. I just laid there taking in every second of it not wanting to miss a thing. Every few minutes or so I kissed Stephanie's forehead, just because I could. After about a half hour of this Stephanie spoke up.

"Why are you still awake?"

"I can't sleep. Why are you still awake?" I asked.

"I can't sleep either. Why can't you sleep?"

"Because I'm laying next to Stephanie Erin. Why can't you sleep?

48

"Because I'm laying next to Jonas Toutant."

That weekend was a weekend of firsts for us. We didn't know how true it was but we really did live like we were dying. Stephanie had never been to a drive in movie so I took her to the drive in. She had never been on a go-cart before so I bought her as many rides on the go-carts as she wanted. As we walked up the road to the go-carts that late afternoon I said to Stephanie, "You know what? I have so many problems with my life right now, but when I'm with you I can't think of what they are."

"What kind of problems do you have?" she asked.

"That's just it, Stephanie; I'm with you right now so I don't know what they are!"

"We never talk about anything serious."

"There's plenty of time to talk about all the serious stuff. For now, let's just forget about it all and enjoy ourselves."

"I like that idea," she said. As we got closer to the go-carts Stephanie started to get winded. I picked her up and carried her the rest of the way, at which point I got winded too so we both took a breather.

Stephanie had the biggest grin on her face when we finally got onto the go-carts; everyone could see that she was having the time of her life. She was the one speeding ahead of everyone else, with the wind in her hair and the blinding sunset on the horizon. It would soon be dark.

Earlier that day when Stephanie and I went downstairs for breakfast my Aunt Elva had us pose for a picture. We held each other in front of the old fireplace. It's now one of my favorite pictures of the two of us. After that picture was taken Stephanie and I went to the boardwalk to look around. We played arcade games, rode the bumper cars, and took pictures together in a photo booth which became my other favorite picture of us. All morning I boasted of my talents at the stuffed animal crane and claw machine game where, using a joystick, you control a crane to hover over a stuffed animal and then drop a claw to grab it out if the machine. Stephanie had seen my collection of winnings from over the years just a week earlier at my apartment and now was my chance to show off my skills; but unfortunately, I was failing miserably! At every machine she would point out what she wanted yet every time I would fail. She was becoming disappointed and I was becoming upset! It wouldn't be until late in the afternoon that I finally won her what she wanted. We had gone for a walk with my family to another arcade up the street from the cottage, and this place was awesome! Aside from Ski Ball (which is by far my favorite arcade game) they had a rock wall! I had never been on a rock wall so Stephanie and I jumped (or I should say climbed) at the opportunity. What ensued was pathetic to say the least. We decided to race to the top and in my haste I fell off after the first step. I decided to take my time; meanwhile Stephanie made it to the top and back down before I even got to the top. I was one step away from the top and I suddenly got scared. I have always been uneasy with heights, but I was right there; just one more step and a stretch of my arm and I'd be able to ring the bell. I had come too far to let my hesitations stop me from doing it. It is said that one of the saddest thing in life is to pull the reins on your horse just before it's about to leap. I wanted that something more. I took that extra step and rang the bell.

The supervisor yelled up to me, "Now just fall!"

"What!" I yelled, "Just fall!?!"

"Yeah, just fall on down," he yelled back.

I was leery of this idea and began instead to carefully move slowly down the same way I went up, which was proving difficult. But then I did it. I finally let go. I just let go and allowed myself to fall. The sensation was amazing! Gently gliding back down to the ground was at one thrilling and frightening! I started kicking my feet back and forth and nearly kicked him in the head! I landed flat on the ground, straight on my back, laughing hysterically!

The climb put Stephanie out; she was completely winded and could barely move let alone stand up. Her body was exhausted. We sat her down at a table nearby. For the past month Stephanie had been experiencing shortness of breath and it had been getting worse and worse. "You really need to get that checked out Stephanie," I said.

"I know, but I think it's just asthma, I must have developed it over the summer. Besides the health insurance at my new job doesn't kick in until next month. I'll make an appointment then." I ran upstairs to get her a bottle of water. There was a sense of urgency in my movements and actions. She was fine. She was going to be ok. I kept telling myself that but I raced as fast as I could. I became winded too. When I came back down she was looking at one of the crane/claw machines. "I want the bear," Stephanie said pointing at a bear wearing purple overalls with a pink heart on its belly.

"This is my chance!" I thought to myself. "All right Stephanie, it's yours!" I put the money in and right on my first try the claw wrapped around the bear and brought it up. The claw opened to let to drop it into the bin below but the bear clung to the claw! I pushed the machine back and forth

but the bear wouldn't budge. This was not fair! I finally get it and now it won't let go! I raced upstairs to talk with an employee about the issue.

"The animal grabby machine won't give me the bear!" Surprisingly the man knew what I was talking about.

"Oh yeah, that bear has a magnet in it and it sticks to the claw, I'll be right down to get it out for you," he said. All of a sudden it didn't seem very impressive. I felt like I was cheating now that I knew there was a magnet involved. If I had just gotten the claw anywhere near the bear it would have picked it up! At least I had finally won Stephanie her prize.

"You're making good on your promises," she said with the bear in her arms.

"I'm a man of my word."

My Uncle Charlie was now at the same claw machine trying to win a prize for his wife Mary. "Are you up for putting on a little magic show for some of the neighbors tomorrow night?" My uncle lives in his RV seasonally at Weirs Beach and got the cottage for us that weekend. The least I could do is share a little magic with the locals.

"Sure," I said, "just tell me when and I'll be there."

I recalled how just two nights earlier at *Samuel's Sports Bar* in downtown Springfield I was in exceptionally good form. I had been working at Eddie Grimaldi's bar every Thursday night for over a year already and was always a night I looked forward to. While visiting with Stephanie the night before she gave me two pictures of her that I kept in my business card wallet. I was able to look at her every time I handed out my cards that night, and I was giving out a lot of cards just so I could look at her. At one point during the evening a gentleman at the bar fell in love with my magic and asked me to perform at his brother's wedding reception being held that weekend.

"Sorry," I said, "but I'll be out of town all this weekend."

"Cancel it," he said, "Triple your fee, I'll pay it; I want you at my brother's wedding." This guy was serious. Then I took out the pictures of Stephanie.

"You don't understand," I said holding up her picture, "this is the love of my life and I'm spending the weekend with her. No amount of money can keep me from that."

"I'll talk to her for you..."

"No you're not, thank you anyway," I said quickly and moved on to the next group.

Just before I left for the night I went outside and spoke with Junior, one of the bouncers. He was having a rough night and needed a little inspiration. I knew what would do the trick. Just a couple weeks earlier I put together a routine inspired by Stephanie, a version of the *Hundred Dollar Bill Trick* used to inspire and motivate others to dream big and to go after those dreams; for Stephanie was my hundred dollar bill. I saw the smile come across his face as I shared the piece with him, and watched the "aha!" moment click.

"I needed this tonight," he said. "You are absolutely right. I just have to keep dreaming and keep going after it. Thank you for that. You don't realize how much I needed to hear this tonight." Even though she was at home sleeping, through me Stephanie was at work inspiring others.

It was Sunday, just before the fireworks, on our last full day at the lake that I was summoned to perform for the locals. Stephanie sat right in the front row just to my left. It was so wonderful having her there laughing and smiling as I performed. Even though I was on vacation, as a magician I always have to be prepared to perform; it's the nature of the business. I had just enough on me to do a solid half hour of material ending with my famous *Houdini Card Trick of Death!* It's actually not famous at all, except for anyone who has seen my act. Interestingly it is also the piece I was going to perform at my audition for *America's Got Talent* the year earlier. It starts off as a simple card trick but takes an interesting turn when I get tied up in a chair and must first escape from the ropes before finding the participant's card. It's a comedy piece where I keep pulling my hands out from under the jacket that covers my bound hands and knees. On this particular night every time I pulled my hands out Stephanie immediately jumped up and pulled my jacket away! So I had to quickly put my hands back before she could and each time I'd still be tied tightly. I can still see her smiling face, sitting there in the front row, just to my left. "How are you doing that!?!" she yelled. She didn't really want to know. She never wanted to know my secrets.

At the end of the show I wrapped up by saying, "It has been a pleasure sharing my magic with all of you. I want to thank you all," pausing, "for making me work on vacation. But seriously, I really enjoyed myself; with my family here and my girlfriend in the audience," we had not yet announced our engagement. "It really has been a pleasure. And I hope that you've enjoyed being a part of the magic as much as I have had sharing it with you. Thank you and goodnight!"

Stephanie came up to me right away and I asked, "Did you enjoy the show? What did you think?"

"I loved it," she said, "I want to be at all of your magic shows!"

56

"You can be if you want to."

As a thank you for sharing my magic with them, the community had a special surprise for me. Every evening they fire off a Civil War cannon on the lawn facing the lake, and not just anyone is permitted to light the wick. That night they bestowed that honor to me! They led me outside where I was instructed to yell *"Fire in the hole!"* and light the wick then run to the side. I love new experiences!

"Fire in the hole!" I yelled, lit the wick then ran and wrapped my arms around Stephanie.

"BOOOOOOM!!!!!!!!"

The noise shook the whole street! They had used more gun powder than usual that night. Always exceptional! Everyone was preparing for the fireworks and our cottage was right across the street from the beach so we had the perfect spot on the second floor porch to watch the display. Stephanie and I hung around outside the cottage by my car for a little while before the display, joking around and having some fun.

"I'm attracted to you like a bug to a bug zapper!" she said suddenly with a smile.

"What!?!" I said "A bug to a bug zapper! You come to me and then die! That's the first analogy that came to mind?"

"Yeah!" she said laughing, "It really was the first thing that came to mind!" We just laughed

57

and laughed at the absurdity of it. It's as if she knew the storm was almost upon us.

The fireworks were beautiful. Stephanie had never been so close to fireworks in all of her life and she was awestruck by them. I held her wrapped in a blanket in my arms to keep her warm. Everything else had vanished and for a moment it was just her, me, and the fireworks. It felt like it would never end.

But that was it. Our time was over. Back home the next day as we pulled onto the exit off 91 South, Stephanie said, "That's it. It's all over."

I stayed for dinner that night. I had spent every moment with Stephanie for the past three days and I didn't want it to end. I let Stephanie keep the picture of us that my aunt had taken by the fireplace. It was such a beautiful picture; I wanted her to have it. The time for me to leave came much too soon. We held each other on the sidewalk outside her house. "I'm going to miss you," I said, "I don't know how I'm going to be able to sleep without you tonight."

"Just live in the moment and enjoy." I smiled at the line, for she had taken a page from my book. What I was always trying to teach Stephanie was, in the end, what she had to teach me.

"You're right Stephanie; and what a wonderful moment it is." That moment still

58

exists. I go back to it from time to time, anytime I want to. I suppose, though, that's living in the past, isn't it?

We kept pulling each other back for one last kiss; one last embrace. We looked into each other's eyes for the last time. What was it that our souls were always saying to each other? In a way we knew then as we always knew even though we didn't know it. As she turned and walked away I took a picture in my mind of that moment just before she closed the door behind her. Her blonde hair was down. She wore a light grey sweatshirt. I took the picture of her in my mind, just in case. An everlasting memory for the moment to live in. Friends, like the days, may come and go; but that still frame in my mind will remain as long as I am aware of myself.

CHAPTER 17
— Connecting The Dots —

*W*e cannot connect the dots looking forward; it is only in looking back that we can see how all the actions of our past directed us to where we are in the present. Likewise, we do not realize why we do something until we do it. For what we plan on doing is not nearly as important as what actually happens; rather our intentions are only a means to an end. In my case I found that becoming a magician was the means to bring Stephanie and I back together.

The first dot I found was as a small boy watching David Copperfield perform the impossible and I began performing magic myself, continuing to perform throughout my high school years. It was of course in high school that I met Stephanie, but being a year ahead of me she went off to college and I was left to finish high school. We tried to stay in touch but with her studies and the craziness of my senior year we lost touch rather quickly. Even though I was only seventeen and didn't know much about love, I knew that I loved Stephanie with everything that I knew of it. *"But I guess it's just not meant to be,"* I reasoned.

When I was nine years old my parents gave me a saxophone and it quickly became one of my deepest passions. After high school people told me I wanted to be a music teacher so I went to UMASS Dartmouth to study music. I wanted to get away from the home I had always known and to explore my new found freedom. The decision was not made lightly. Having received a full teaching scholarship I did not have to pay a dime for tuition, however I did have to pay for everything else, including housing. Without much money I couldn't afford housing on campus so I lived in my van in the local Stop and Shop parking lot near the university. The Stop and Shop offered twenty-four hour access which was a big plus. It was during this interesting time in my life that I stumbled upon the magic marketing materials of Dave Dee and I studied them closely. Having nothing but time on my hands I worked tirelessly to market my magic business between classes, studying, practicing the saxophone and sleeping in my van down by the river.

This situation was working well until the weather turned cold. After only two frozen nights I made the move on campus to Lot 10, just behind the Visual and Performing Arts building. This had some nice advantages. The gym was nearby, just across the street from my new parking space. Every morning I could simply walk across the street and use the facilities to start my day. Also, if I managed to sneak into the Visual and

Performance Arts building before it was locked for the evening I had a warm place to sleep and could stay up practicing my saxophone all through the night. This lasted only a year before I tired of the lifestyle. I moved back home and transferred to Westfield State College to continue my studies. This situation was far more ideal and I continued to market my business, create original performance material, perform magic shows and also began teaching private music lessons, all between my studies and working part-time at a local grocery store. The rigorous schedule was catching up to me but I never gave up. Obstacles threatened to stop me but I refused to give in. That is until finishing my sophomore year at Westfield State.

The Commonwealth of Massachusetts was making cutbacks and Governor Romney thought that the scholarship program should be one of the first things to go. I was left at a crossroad: Do I apply for financial aid and students loans? Or do I leave school and finally pursue my magic career full-time? I realized that by going to music school I was buying into other people's version of reality. I went there because that's what I was told I wanted. *"You can't make a living with magic anyway"* everyone told me, even other magicians. *"It's not easy"* they would say. I believed them for years until I realized I had taken a wrong turn.

Music school wasn't for me; I wanted to be a magician. It may not be easy but for me it's worth it. The idea of focusing all of my efforts on this one goal seemed like a great idea. Instead of having what seemed like a hundred different things to focus on I could channel my full attention to jumpstarting my business. *"We get what we focus on,"* I remembered. After two years of college I left in pursuit of my childhood dream. Turns out that was the best decision I had ever made, for a reason I was unaware of then.

I soon joined the Society of American Magician's Assembly #17 in Springfield, MA. Our assembly does several shows a year as fundraisers for other organizations in the Springfield area and it was in December 2004 that we held one such event. It was for a Boy Scout troop in Agawam. The whole club was involved. Whether it was stage time or taking the role as stage manager, manning the curtain, or running the sound system, everyone had a job. Dave Xanatos was running the sound system that night. That evening I performed my *Houdini Card Trick of Death!* routine. Dave liked it. After the show he approached me and asked if I'd be willing to share the method with him.

"Of course," I said, "Come by my office Monday afternoon and I'll teach it to you." I liked being able to say that. *"Come by my office."* In an

63

effort to separate my home life from my work I rented a cheap space in a local office building to serve as my magic studio. When Dave came to the office that Monday he was impressed with the operation. I wasn't treating magic as a hobby, rather as a business. As a self-employed businessman himself, Dave appreciated that. He looked around the room. Various magic props randomly on display; books of every genre in no particular order thrown on shelves; a cluttered desk of folders and invoices; and above the desk hung a bulletin board. What was on the bulletin board is what caught Dave's eye.

"Did you perform those eleven magic shows?" Dave was looking at my goals posted prominently on the bulletin board.

"Nope, they never happened." The goal sheet stated: *"Goal for November: perform fifteen magic shows...11 to go!"* November had been a slow month, as it had been every year before.

"Would you like to reach your goals?" Dave asked in the way that he so often does when already knowing the answer. He is a master of NLP (Neuro-Linguistic Programming).

I took the bait, "Yes, I would like to reach my goals. What do you have in mind?"

"Let's talk over dinner," he said.

The dinner was riveting and the conversation delicious. I was hooked. I agreed to join the networking group that Dave belonged to, Business Networking International. BNI offered me the opportunity to meet with local business owners every week to educate them on my business and in turn to learn about their businesses. It took me several months to save up enough money to join the local Ludlow BNI Chapter but in April, 2005 I took the risk and dove in. Four short months later I had enough business coming in to quit my job at the local grocery store. It was August and I had just turned twenty-two.

Our chapter's networking meetings were held every Tuesday at 7AM sharp. We got the opportunity to get to know members of our group and we could also visit other chapters of the organization as substitutes for other members who could not make their own meetings. Attendance at the meetings was mandatory with the penalty of expulsion from the group if you didn't have a substitute. Very strict, but it ensures that members in the chapter are committed to each other's success. Taking advantage of the substitute program I was averaging three to four sales meetings a week, getting my name and face in front of hundreds of business professionals and potential clients. Leveraging my time at these meetings not only brought in more business than I ever dreamed of but it also aligned me as the "go-to" guy whenever a client needed something.

I became indispensable and I had retained a much larger percentage of clients as a result. It was at one of these networking meetings in January 2006 that would connect all the dots along the way to reveal the beautiful picture fate had in mind.

I was at one of the rare 5:30PM BNI meetings when I thought I recognized one of the members, Brian, an insurance agent. But how did I know Brian? I didn't have a chance to approach him that week and so the following week I again looked at him quizzically. *"Why do I recognize this guy?"* I thought. Nothing clicked. At the end of that meeting I had an opportunity to personally introduce myself just as the meeting ended. I approached him. "Brian, how do I know you?"

"You know my daughter," he answered.

"Who's your daughter?"

His answer made my heart race, "Stephanie."

I frantically put my hands in my pockets; I couldn't get my business card out and into his hands fast enough. "Really! Stephanie! That's awesome!" I tried to control my excitement but was failing miserably. "Tell her to give me a call, you know, if she wants to." I was trying to play it cool. Over the five years that we had lost touch I tried searching for her. I sent emails to old email addresses and called old phone numbers. I paid for "find-a-friend" and "classmate" services online but nothing worked. Stephanie, it seemed, was lost to me forever. But that was not the fate that was meant to be. A week later my phone rang: it was Stephanie. After five years of being apart Stephanie was back in my life and we picked up right where we had left off. The dots lead us back together.

CHAPTER 18
— Planning The Speech —
September 4, 2007

I decided to sleep in. Stephanie was back at work after the three day weekend and I didn't have anything to do until band practice that night. When I woke up I went for my daily jog. Daily is a term used loosely; I had been jogging every day for the past five months but I had taken a week off when my foot started bothering me. After only a few days it started to feel better but then my leg started bothering me. When I told Stephanie this she explained that "One pain replaces another." I suppose that is too often true.

My leg was feeling ok today so I put on my new running shoes and set out. It was a hot day but with a cool breeze perfect for running. My thoughts turned to Stephanie immediately. I remembered the story she told me about when her grandparents got engaged. They had only been together for six weeks when her grandfather proposed. Six weeks from August twenty-sixth would be October seventh; I decided that would be the day that I would give Stephanie her ring. The ring I still didn't have. That would be top priority.

My imagination went wild scheming how I'd give Stephanie her ring. Stephanie liked hot air balloons but had never been in one. In my mind October seventh was to be a beautiful day, with bright blue skies and white fluffy clouds. Stephanie and I would be in a hot air balloon. I'd tell her a couple of jokes.

Joke One:

There was this young man praying to God. He wanted to win the lottery but every day would come and pass without any winnings. He prayed more and more every day but it was to no avail. Prayers unanswered the young man became frustrated and in his anger yelled, "Lord! You said that anything I asked for would be given, so why have you not answered my prayers to win the lottery!?!"

Just then a bright light shown down on the man and a booming voice came down from the heavens, "Meet me half way! Buy a lottery ticket!"

Joke Two:

A young woman was on a cruise ship. One day the ship sank suddenly and the woman was the sole survivor, laying desperately on a shabby raft. The woman prayed to God to be saved.

One day a boat came to rescue her, but she refused their help. "The good Lord will save me," she said faithfully.

The next day another boat came by but she said the same thing, "The good Lord will save me."

On the third day she was weak from exhaustion, having not eaten in days and unable to sleep. The woman prayed more and more for God to save her from her plight. A third ship came to her rescue but she again sent them away refusing their help.

She died later that day. When she got to heaven and met God the woman asked Him, "Lord, you said that whatever I asked for would be given. Why, when I needed you the most, did you not save me?"

Frustrated, God answered, "I sent you three boats, what more did you want?"

After telling those jokes I would point to a cloud and make it disappear. I learned how to do that trick just a month earlier from Devin Knight's and Jerome Finley's book *Cloud Busting Secrets*. Now would be the perfect time to perform what I had learned. Then I would again talk of the dance I took her to all those years ago and what she had said to me that night. *"If you want to dance with me all you have to do is ask."* Then with ring in hand I'd say, "I want to dance with you for the rest of my life."

Yes, October seventh was going to be a wonderful day. Not a doubt about it. But it was still only September fourth. I had run my four mile route back to my apartment without even realizing it. I was not the least bit tired so I kept going. I had more things to think about. My magic career was doing great. Every year my business was growing bigger and better and my material was becoming really solid as my character became much more defined. Having just finished the financially best summer I had ever had my bills were paid up to the end of the year, I had more money put away in my bank account than I had ever had and I had gigs lined up for the months ahead and calls still coming in. I had struggled for years to get to where I was now and I was finally living my dream as a successful full-time performing magician. But I had in my hands the manifestation of another dream. A greater dream. The dream of a life shared with Stephanie. The entertainment industry is not an easy career for personal relationships and I wasn't going to let anything get in our way. I was giving up magic. The thought was almost laughable. I had been so sure of my life's path for so long, since I was a child, and yet here I was giving it up. Stephanie didn't ask it of me, I wasn't doing it for her; I was doing it for me. Stephanie was my greatest magic trick of all. My biggest, most wildest dream.

They say that love will make you do crazy things yet even the absurdity of giving up magic made perfect sense to me. I had been focused on one goal my whole life without knowing why; suddenly the answer stared me in the face. Looking back it could be said that the only reason I became a magician was to bring Stephanie and I together and, having accomplished that, there was no reason left to continue on being a magician. My dots proved that. I wasn't giving up on a dream rather I was giving up the life I had been planning to accept the life that was waiting for me. We do not realize why we do things until we do it.

CHAPTER 19
— Goodnight —
September 4, 2007

*F*inished the eight-mile jog just in time to get Stephanie's call. She had just gotten out of work. I told her nothing of my plans; it would be a surprise. I showered and dressed, grabbed my saxophone and left for the jewelry store. Later that night I would be going to my first rehearsal with a band I had just joined. The Mojos are a cover band that plays the greatest hits from the fifties all the way to contemporary top charts hits, and I was their latest saxophonist. I took any and all opportunities to jam with local musicians so I was excited when asked to join them. But I was now kicking myself for making that decision. I didn't feel like going to band practice; I wanted to go see Stephanie. I almost called and told them that I couldn't make it but Stephanie said that I shouldn't cancel. She told me I'd be able to see her tomorrow.

When I arrived at the jewelry store I looked through the lettering on the glass door and grabbed the handle and pulled it open.

"Am I really doing this?" I thought to myself. *"Am I actually coming into this store to pick out an engagement ring? Yes! I am! And it's for Stephanie*

73

Erin!" My heart raced as I sat down at the glass counter, staring starry eyed at the glimmering diamonds listening to Denise Quinn, the owner, explain the various subtle variations to choose from. *"I'm actually doing this!"* I smiled the whole time like a lunatic.

I knew what I was looking for. Just two weeks earlier Stephanie told me that her favorite playing card was the Three of Clubs. Knowing that a week later I tried to do a card trick for her assuming that she would select the Three of Clubs. But she didn't; she picked the Three of Diamonds instead. I was puzzled. "Why the Three of Diamonds?" I asked.

"Because that's the kind of ring that I want," she said. Yeah, she always knew how to get what she wanted.

"May I see that one please?" My eyes went straight to it, almost as if I had seen it before. It was simple yet elegant. The light sparkled through the three mounted diamonds. Denise handed it to me and I held as if I had held it a hundred times before. I knew right away that it was Stephanie's ring. But I needed to find out her ring size so I had it placed aside and I left with plans to return a couple days later. *"I have until October seventh anyway,"* I thought to myself, *"no rush."*

The Mojos are a tight group. They've been around for a while and each individual member is a veteran of the local music scene. I had never been to the house before and as I walked in through the garage I could hear that they were listening to a CD of one of the songs that they cover. When I entered the living room I was shocked to see that they weren't listening to a CD at all; they were actually playing the music themselves! *"This is going to be fun!"*

Yet my mind was elsewhere. I could think of nothing but Stephanie. We played for several hours and it was starting to get late. I kept looking to my cell phone. I had asked Stephanie to call me before she went to bed so that I could say goodnight to her. It was almost 10:30PM when we played *Can't Take My Eyes off of You*. I closed my eyes as we played and saw Stephanie. The song was right; I couldn't take my eyes off of her. When we stopped to fix a section of the song I took the opportunity to look at my phone. Stephanie had called! At 10:31PM! And I missed it! But she left a message. Without saying a word to the band I ran outside to listen to her message. It was a sweet message. It made me smile. The sound of her voice. So soft. So tired. She was laying in bed just about to sleep. I saved it so I could listen to it again and again. I had two other voicemails from her that I had saved and listen to every now and again, just to hear the sound of her voice. I had to hurry up and call Stephanie before she was asleep! It was 10:38PM.

Stephanie answered quietly. Sweetly. It was a simple call. We talked about her, we talked about me and we talked about how happy we were. We talked about our plans to move to Connecticut to be closer to her work. And that was it. It was a short call for soon after the singer from the band came outside, "We're going to play one more song then we're going to call it a night."

"Ok," I hollered back. "Stephanie, I have to go back inside and play one more song with the band."

"That's ok, I know you're busy," Stephanie said softly, "I'm tired anyway and have to go to sleep. I have work to do tomorrow."

"Ok Stephanie, I love you. Sleep well. I hope you have sweet dreams."

"They'll be sweet if they're of you." I loved it when she said that.

"I'll call you in the morning and talk to you on your way to work. I love you."

"I love you too Jonas, goodnight. Bye baby."

"I love you too, goodnight." Stephanie and I always had a hard time ending our phone conversations. We would always keep saying goodbye over and over and then wait to hang up until the other did. We were so cute it was pathetic. But tonight was different. Stephanie hung up the phone right away. *"She must be really tired"* I thought to myself. Back inside we played *Suspicious Minds* and it reminded me of the Elvis lookalike that I met at *LaNotte Restaurante* just a month earlier and the choking woman who was with him. Remembering the lesson her story taught me, the puzzle pieces were finally fitting into place and it was easy to see the beautiful picture it would soon reveal.

By the time I got back to my apartment and settled into bed it was well after midnight. I was just about to lie down to sleep when my cell phone rang. It was my mother. *"Calling at this hour it must be an emergency!"* I thought to myself. I ran outside onto the porch to take her call.

"Mom! What's wrong?" I asked.

"Nothing," she said in her motherly way, "I couldn't sleep and I was worried about you for some reason and I just wanted to make sure you were ok. I figured you'd still be awake."

"Yeah, you know my schedule, I never sleep," I replied. "Everything is fine. Great actually." My mother has always had a knack for knowing exactly when something important was about to happen. It's almost like a premonition. She often told the story of the time when she was a teenager out on a date with her boyfriend and she suddenly got the feeling that she needed to go home. She made her boyfriend drive her back home quickly and when she got there she found out that her grandfather had just passed away. I told my mother every detail of the weekend Stephanie and I had together, and about my trip to the jewelry store.

"It sounds like you're pretty serious."

"Yes I am," I said, "I have been in love with Stephanie for a long time; I can hardly believe that this is actually happening! Can you believe it? In my whole life I've only ever really wanted two things: to become a magician and to be with Stephanie, and today I have both! I feel guilty! Why should I be so lucky?"

"You're lucky because you've worked hard all of these years. I always knew you'd get anything you wanted; I always told you that you could do and be anything you wanted. Remember me telling you that when you were a child?"

"Yes, I do remember that," I said, "but hearing it and actually living it is totally different." My mother always did believe in me. It's amazing when these things actually happen though; when everything you were told about clicks into place. We only talked for a short while. I was tired and ready to sleep.

I laid down into bed and looked over to the nightstand. There was Stephanie and I, in the picture we took in the photo booth.

78

"Goodnight Stephanie!" I said turning off the light.

Then I turned the light back on.

"I'll talk to you in the morning!" I turned the light off.

I turned the light back on.

"I miss you Stephanie! I love you!"

I turned the light back off then quickly turned it back on.

"I can't take my eyes off of you."

CHAPTER 20
— Waking Up Is The Hardest Part —
September 5, 2007

Woke up to the sound of the alarm clock. Rubbed my eyes, glanced at the clock. 7:01AM. Time to call Stephanie. I rolled out of bed, picked up my cell phone and sat down at my desk, still half asleep. The phone rang and rang but Stephanie did not pick up. *"Hi, you have reached Stephanie. I'm not available at the moment so please leave a message. Thank you."*

"Hi Stephanie, it's me, Jonas. Just calling to say good morning. I hope you slept well last night and that you have a great day at work today. I love you, I miss you. Give me a call when you get a chance. I love you. Bye."

I spoke with an unusually sweet tone that took me by surprise, especially for that early in the morning. This magician usually doesn't take kindly to mornings. I laid down back in bed and dosed off a bit more before waking up a minutes later to call Stephanie again. No answer. Didn't leave a message that time. Slept some more then woke up and called her one last time. Again no answer. She must have overslept, I thought. Or maybe she's running late for work and can't talk, I imagined. Or maybe she forgot her cell phone at home, I reasoned. Whatever it was I knew she'd call back later, I hoped.

You always prepare yourself for bad things to happen but you never actually expect them to. Just the week earlier I had noticed that one of the tires on Stephanie's car was a bit low on air. "You have to get that fixed," I told her, "I wouldn't be able to live with myself if anything bad happened to you." I was on the phone with her the next day when she was on her way home from work. She was pulling into an auto service station for an oil change. "And to get your tire fixed," I reminded her. I needed to know that she was safe, and what safer place to be than in the comfort of your own home sleeping? Then again, Stephanie was always the exception. She was exceptional.

Later that tired morning I'd get a phone call from her mother and I'd rush over to find the police cars. She would tell me that she had never seen Stephanie as happy as she was the night before, telling of all the fun she and I had that weekend.

"Do you love him?" she asked Stephanie.

"Yes." I was told that she was beaming.

I realized then that I had gotten exactly what I had prayed for. Stephanie was happy for the rest of her life; it was just a very short life. Without warning, that was the morning Stephanie died.

CHAPTER 21
— Just Yesterday Morning—
September 6, 2007

Woke up at 8:56AM. Looked to the nightstand. There she was, smiling in the photograph. Lay motionless in bed for a time then picked up my phone and called her. Heard her cell phone ring from my desk. Somehow I had acquired it during the events of the day before. *"That was supposed to have been a dream,"* I thought. Looked at her phone. She had a text message from an unknown number. *"I just heard a terrible rumor that you are dead. Please text me and tell me that it isn't true."* For a moment I thought about replying, *"No, it's true. I'm dead."* But that would have been a bit much.

I still couldn't feel anything but the tingling sensation was now gone. The day before I sat in the love seat in Stephanie's living room where just days earlier we had sat together. Not wanting to accept what had happened my whole body fell asleep and the tingling sensation felt like needles were sticking inside me poking from the inside out.

Got out of bed and put on one my favorite CD's, the *Poems, Prayers and Promises* album by John Denver. On it John Denver covers a James Taylor song that for some reason I had always related to although it never much made sense until now. *"Just yesterday morning they let me know you were gone..."* I cried uncontrollably. *"I've seen fire and I've seen rain. I've seen sunny days that I thought would never end. I've seen lonely times when I could not find a friend. But I always thought I'd see you again."*

CHAPTER 22
— Nothing More To Say —

*E*veryone was gathered around today
With the sun shining through leaves of the dell;
It was beautiful, what more can I say?

We gathered to honor you and to pray
For your journey on, and to say farewell;
Everyone was gathered around today!

As they all spoke of you I looked your way;
You were smiling with a love we know well,
It was beautiful, what more can I say?

I became confused; I thought that I may
Have been dreaming it. Then I heard the bell...
Everyone was gathered around today.

I looked to you but you had gone away,
Rather a lone box lay were the leaves fell.
It was beautiful, what more can I say?

Just a dream. This is your funeral today;
I miss you more than I can ever tell.
Everyone was gathered around today;
It was beautiful, nothing more to say.

CHAPTER 23
— The Ring —

I had cancelled all of my performances for the past two weeks. All, that is, save for one. It was a cancer benefit for a local woman that her family had put together in her memory. This would be my second year in a row performing for them and I knew that Stephanie would have wanted me to be there to help bring smiles, laughter and mystery to the young and young at heart. It had only been four days since my world turned dark and later that day I'd be going to Stephanie's wake. I hadn't seen Stephanie since the night we got back from our vacation and I really wasn't looking forward to seeing her at the funeral parlor, even though I had a gift for her. Her friend had given me Stephanie's ring size and so the day after she died I went back to the jewelry store and picked up her ring. I had promised her the ring and I was determined to do so even now.

The magic was a blur, though I do remember performing with a smile even through the tears. I also remember a band was playing and I got my saxophone out of the car and played with them. I was wearing sunglasses so they couldn't tell that I was crying as the music poured like sweat out of me.

It was an unimaginable Sunday afternoon when I stepped through the unfathomable door of the funeral parlor and walked the impossible walk across the floral scented room and stood over Stephanie's lifeless body lying in her casket. There I was with ring in hand finally ready to give it to her, when I saw in my heart that the woman lying in that casket was not Stephanie.

No.

It was not my best friend.

No.

It was not her.

No.

It was most certainly the body her soul inhabited during her time as Stephanie but no, it was not Stephanie.

And so I couldn't give Stephanie's ring to the lifeless body that was not her and so I kept it, carrying her ring with me anywhere and everywhere I went in search of her from appletini to appletini yet anywhere and everywhere I could not find her. I drank all my work. I drank all my possessions. I drank all my money. I drank all my hopes. I drank all my life away and still I couldn't find her. The storm was now directly overhead and all hope was loster than lost.

CHAPTER 24
— Back To Work —

*M*issed enough work. Time to go back. It was a street festival in my hometown that I found myself making balloon sculptures. I hate making balloon sculptures. I strapped a smile around my face and put the balloon belt on my waist and stood in the middle of the street, doing nothing but waiting for someone to ask for a balloon even though I wanted to be left alone. That's when the little girl came up to me. Her voice was little and was soft in height. What she asked for made my smile genuine.

"Will you please make me and angel?"

I had never made a balloon angel before let alone even seen one made.

"Have you ever seen a balloon angel before?" I asked.

"No," she replied.

"But you would like one."

"Yes."

"Ok, coming right up." It took me several minutes to do. How do you make something you've never seen before? But I made an angel for that little girl, just as Stephanie had asked her to ask me to make. Complete with halo and all.

Stephanie so loved butterflies, that's why I wasn't surprised by what happened a week later at another festival, this time in Granby. I was in no mood. No mood at all to put the happy face on again. But as I got set up for the show I remembered what Stephanie had said to me just weeks earlier. She had sat in the front row, just to my left, as I performed for the locals at the lake. When she came up to me after the show she said, "I want to be at all of your magic shows." Now more than ever Stephanie truly can be at all of my magic shows, and I cannot disappoint. As I started my performance I imagined that Stephanie was again sitting in the second row, just to my left. Halfway through my opening lines I looked over to where I was imagining she would be, and there she was! A beautiful butterfly fluttering in place. A very special guest indeed.

CHAPTER 25
— Death Follows Me —

*J*ust days before I was born my parents went for a walk through a cemetery to look at the tombstones to pick out a name for me. When they saw the name "Jonas" they knew right away that it was my name. Then they gave me the middle name Cain, as in the first killer. It's an interesting combination considering Jonas Cain means "Creator of Peace." At the age of eight I wondered what it would be like to be dead and contemplated killing myself just so I could find out. When I was eleven I fell running up the steps to my home and received a serious head injury and I was told that if I landed just a couple of inches off I would have died. A year later while at the beach the ocean waves pulled me out too far. Had it not been for my cousin Rachel who was with me I would have drowned. She was just a tad bit taller than me and was able to pull us both back to shore with her big toe. A year later at the age of thirteen I was performing in my high school's variety show with my version of acid roulette, using real Hydrochloric Acid. Accidentally swallowing the acid live on stage nearly killed me. That's the same year I put my father's gun to my head. Perhaps the acid roulette was a death wish. Whenever I heard news of someone's death I would smile. Perhaps it was an uncomfortable smile or maybe it I was that I was happy for them, knowing that they finally got to find out what death is like. Or perhaps it was a jealous smile. People would call me on it; they would ask, *"Why are you smiling? Are you happy they're dead?"* The smile was taken from my face the day Stephanie died and now more than ever death is all that I long for. Indeed, death follows me.

CHAPTER 26
— A Dream —

Had a dream that I was laying in bed with Stephanie, holding her in my arms. I held her that way for months and months, refusing to let go and refusing to do anything else. Then one day she said to me, "Jonas, this is ridiculous. You have to let me go of me, I'm dead!"

I thought about it for a moment then said, "You're right, I should. You're really starting to smell."

Even in my dreams I'm absurd.

CHAPTER 27
— Everything's Perfect —
October 6 – 7, 2007

I started going crazy. I convinced myself that I would die today. Mathematically it just made sense. It was a full month and a day from when Stephanie had died. From August third, our lovely evening together on the park bench, to September fifth was a full month and a day. October seventh, a full month and a day after Stephanie died and six weeks from the day Stephanie and I became a couple. October seventh, the day I planned to give Stephanie her ring in the hot air balloon. I had planned for this day; I wrote it into my schedule back on September fourth. *"I'm going to do it."* I did not write, *"Give Stephanie her ring,"* oh no; I wrote, *"I'm going to do it."* That left it open ended; it meant I was going to do it. I was going to kill myself.

I had several gigs the day before. I treated them as if they were my last so there was no need to hand out any more business cards. One woman did ask for a card though and I laughed when I handed it to her. *"What's the point?"* After the first run of shows I went back to my apartment and watched a DVD that I had just received in the mail, *When the Leaves Blow Away.*

It answered the question, *"If today was your last day what would you do with it?"* Stay home and watch a movie, that's what I'd do.

The movie was too much for me to handle. It was Steven Wright's stand-up comedy but his short film *One Soldier* at the end put me over the edge. I drove to the cemetery crying hysterically, collapsing on Stephanie's grave when I got there. I held her ring tightly in my hands with my head face first in the grass and in goose poo. I stayed like that for several minutes before I finally looked up just in time to see a bird fly by. The trees looked beautiful lit by the slowly setting sun. I looked down at her ring. The sunlight glimmered through the diamonds. The thought crossed my mind, *"I'm going to miss being alive."* I drove to the church; wanted to go inside but it was locked up so I sat on a bench outside for several minutes. *"I thought God's house was always open"* I thought to myself. There were ten candles lit and five bugs buzzing around. I stayed just before it got too dark. I still had one more magic show to do. My last one ever.

It was held at the American Legion Pavilion in Monson for the *Children's Miracles Network*. Every year for the past several years I'd donated my time to perform for the event. I pulled my car up and slipped a deck of cards into my pocket along with some sponge balls. I was in no mood to perform. I was in no mood to be alive. Don't remember much from the performance. The only memory I have is sitting at a picnic table outside the pavilion doing a card trick for a young boy and his parents and when I was done I was afforded the opportunity to slip away quietly.

I was surprised when I woke up the next morning. Had expected to pass away quietly in my sleep just as Stephanie has done. But there are twenty-four hours in a day, I reasoned; plenty of time to die. Dark clouds filled the sky with an even drizzle of rain in the early morning. Had two gigs to do that day. A child's birthday party magic show at *Pazzo's Restaurant* in downtown Springfield and Opel was playing at *Pearl Street* in Northampton later that night. Opel has been described as a vaguely folkish rock group, a unique sound with songs of addiction and obsession to letting go and experiencing outside worlds. The music is as fun to play as it is to listen to, especially with my obsession with death and my desire to let go of life to experience the outside world; life in the world beyond. It was the only band I was playing with lately. Having only rehearsed once with the Mojos I did the one gig that I had committed myself to before leaving the group. It just didn't feel right. On the last night of Stephanie's life I spent the time rehearsing with the band instead of being with her. I resented

94

myself for that so I quit the band. Then again she wouldn't have wanted me to be there anyway, to have been there when she left. I started going insane, telling friends that I was "leaving the box." I stopped showering and shaving which gave me the look of a mountain man and I smelt like one too.

Pulled up to the restaurant very early, my show wasn't even to begin for another hour but I had nothing else to do anyway. I set up the equipment for the show and walked outside and sat down on a park bench. I held Stephanie's ring lightly in my hand, looking at how the sunlight shined through it. It reminded me of laying in the goose poo in the cemetery that day before. *"Sunlight,"* I thought and I looked up to the sky. The dark clouds that had been there that morning had disappeared and were replaced by bright blue skies and white fluffy clouds. The weather was perfect, just as I had envisioned during my jog on September fourth, planning how I would give Stephanie her ring. A smile came across my face. Then tears. I went inside. The performance was a blur.

I drove to Northampton without even realizing it. It was the hot air balloons that pulled me out of the daze. I saw them against the blue sky just as I approached the exit ramp off of 91 North. It amazed me; it was exactly what I had seen in my mind a full month and a day before. Everything was perfect. I smiled. Perfect except for the most important part. I screamed, slamming my hands on the steering wheel, crying hysterically.

"I'm going to do it."

I spiraled to the very top of the parking garage, stopping next to the convenient ledge. Grabbing my saxophone from the trunk I looked over the side of the low wall down to the ground. *"That's plenty high,"* I thought to myself. *"Just to be sure I'll land on my head."*

Walked to Pearl Street and met up with the band. I wasn't really there. I tried to take it all in, to live in the moment knowing that this would be my last time with them, with anyone; but I had already let myself go over the edge before it even happened. I'd like to say that I put my heart and soul into that last performance but I don't even remember playing. When we finished our set I put my saxophone away. "I'll be right back guys," I lied, "I just want to put my sax in the car."

"All right, see you when you get back," one of them said.

"It's been a pleasure playing with you guys. Thank you." I shook their hands. Then I left.

You know that feeling you get just before you die? That sense of impending doom yet everything around you seems more inviting than ever? It makes you wish that you didn't have to go yet, makes you wish that you could stay just one more day. Even just one more minute. That's what it felt like during that walk up to the top of the parking garage.

"I'm going to do it."

I put my sax in the trunk and walked to the edge, hoisting myself up. I looked down to the ground then got off the ledge and went back to my car. Sitting in the driver's seat I wrote a Haiku on the back of one of my business cards.

> *Everything happens*
> *for a reason. I take com-*
> *fort in knowing that.*

I wrote, *"I was meant to do this,"* at the bottom then set the mysterious suicide note on the driver's seat and locked the door. *"They'll be able to get in when they find the keys on my body,"* I thought to myself.

I again hoisted myself up onto the ledge and looked down. I closed my eyes and envisioned myself letting go and free falling through the air, just as I had done while rock wall climbing with Stephanie. I experienced the sensation of free falling through my entire body, and it freaked me out so much that I stepped off the ledge. *"I'm going to have to be drunk to do this."* I wandered back to Pearl Street, a dead man walking.

"I'm going to do it."

Looking back I realize that I had already died yet was still alive to grieve my own passing, but it was not a physical death that befell me; rather the death of who I was in order to bring about the birth of who I was to become.

Everything was perfect.

When I got back to the club I collapsed onto the floor and stared a blank stare into nothingness. "Are you all right man?" an older gentleman asked. I simply nodded. In my mind I had already committed the act. I wasn't really there. Stayed just few moments then said my goodbyes and walked across the street to a The Canteen Cave to get drunk.

The Canteen Cave is an interesting place. It's literally built inside of a hill with the entrance on the side of the hill, like the entrance to a cave. Earlier that year I had gone there with Stephanie to celebrate her best friend Lauren's birthday. This was my first time back there since then. I sat at the end of the bar where Stephanie had sat that night. I ordered an appletini and struck up a conversation with a guy named Kevin. It turns out he was the general manager of the bar and the restaurant upstairs. He had the night off because it was his birthday. Appletini after appletini and several hours later I had had plenty of drinks to do what I was resolved to do. I turned around on the bar stool and there was no one left in the bar. It was just the bartender and Kevin and me.

"Where are you parked Jonas?" Kevin asked.

"I'm at the garage," I replied.

"I'll drive you there," he said, "I just have to go to my office to get my brief case. Come on up with me."

We walked up stairs and I excused myself to the bathroom for some much needed relief. When I came out Kevin was standing right by the doorway of the restroom. "You know what you need Jonas?" he said.

"What's that Kevin?"

"A hug."

"You're right, I do," and with that we embraced. That's when he asked the question that changed the whole context of the experience.

"This doesn't make you feel weird does it?"

Picture this if you will: The restaurant is closed and is pitch dark save for the street lights coming in from the windows of the sleeping city. There is no one around except for Kevin and me. I am a well dressed man drinking appletinis at *The Canteen Cave* in Northampton having just spent the whole night talking to this guy named Kevin, and am now hugging him alone in the dark. That's just a little creepy! But I didn't want to offend him so I played it cool.

"No," I said, "it's cool."

We walked slowly to the front of the restaurant in the dark. I just wanted to get out of there but he was walking so slowly, stopping every few steps as he talked about something, I don't even remember what; I just wanted to get out of there! We finally made it to the front of the restaurant and he said, "Just have to grab my briefcase from my office upstairs, come with me."

"I'm staying right here!" I said. I knew if I went upstairs with Kevin into his private office that I would have lost more than my sobriety that night. He ran upstairs and I started pacing in the dark. *"How the hell did I get myself into this situation?"* I wondered to myself. *"Appletinis,"* I concluded. Kevin finally came back downstairs and we walked outside to his car in the parking lot. We sat in his car talking and holding hands. *"Seriously! How did I get myself in this situation!?!"* I thought again. *"Stephanie is probably up there right now laughing her ass off!"* Kevin finally started up his car and drove to the entrance of the parking garage.

"Are you all right to drive?" Kevin asked.

"Of course," I said. Truthfully I wasn't but I just wanted to get the hell out of there.

"Because I'll drive you all the way back to your house if you want," he said.

"Thank you Kevin, but I'll be ok," I replied. It was nice of him to offer, but I didn't want to have to give him any favors for it.

"What route are you taking home?" he asked.

"I'm taking 91 South to the Mass Pike exit 8 in Palmer, that's route 32. I'll follow 32 South all the way into Monson. I'm on the left right next to the bowling alley across from the big white church. Very easy to find." Why I gave him turn-by-turn directions is beyond me. Then he told me that I had a cute button nose, hugged me again, swapped numbers, and then he left.

Finally free! Free so that I can finally do what I came to do! I paid the parking fee then ran up the stairs (it was rather more of a stumble) to the roof of the garage and propped myself back up onto the ledge. I paused there thinking about what had just happened to me. The humor of it all spoke to the comic inside me and I knew that I couldn't die that night. I had to live long enough to tell my friends about the absurd situation I had gotten myself into. I stepped down from the ledge, got into my car and started her up. Drove "Old Bertha", my '94 Buick LeSabre, down the spiral ramp to the gate below. The spiraling down brought to my attention that driving was probably not the best idea realizing how much I had had to drink. The situation spoke again to me, but this time to the suicidal person inside me. Best-case scenario I'd die, that would cross one thing off my to-do list. Worst case I get in trouble with the police. It didn't occur to me then the danger that I had put the other drivers in who were out on the road that night. After pulling out of the garage I started practicing the alphabet, just in case. I was doing fine till I'd get to the middle section. I kept messing up the "LMNOP" part. *"This is not good!"*

Decided to get some food in me so I stopped at the *Fifties Diner* in Chicopee just off exit 6 of the Mass Pike. Pulled into a parking spot and started walking to the entrance when a shadowy figure called over to me.

"Hey you!" he yelled.

"Be right there," I yelled back and started walking in his direction into the shadows. It seemed like a perfectly normal thing to do at 2:30AM. "What can I do for you?" I asked.

The young man proceeded to tell me his story, how he needed to get to work in Deerfield at Yankee Candle but was running out of gas and didn't have any money. I stopped him right there and took out my wallet handing him a twenty. "Will that be enough?" I asked.

"That'll be great!" he said relieved, "Thank you so so much. I'll pay you back."

"That won't be necessary," I said, but he insisted, so for the second time that night I swapped numbers with a dude. Then I said, "What do you see when you see a goose?"

"A creature of God," he replied.

"Well, yes," I said, "but we also see geese. Never just a goose. We have all been put into this life together, if we have any hope of survival we must stick together with our gaggle of family, friends and even complete strangers." He appreciated my philosophy, and the twenty dollars. After saying goodbye I went inside the diner and ordered a sandwich. While waiting for the meal I read the funny papers. There were two frames that caught my eye which were simply entitled "*Perfect*". The first frame depicted a young, beautiful woman laying in a grassy meadow and the frame below had this simple poem:

> *Lying in this meadow*
> *This Indian Summer afternoon*
> *All my minutes stretch to hours,*
> *And the sun sets too soon.*
> *The cool breeze brushes by me*
> *Like I'm not even here at all.*
> *Perfect.*
> *Life is perfect...*
> *In this meadow, early fall.*

When I got to the line *"the sun sets too soon"* I began to cry; and when it came to *"like I'm not even there at all"* I lost it completely. Yes, October 7, 2007 was perfect, complete with bright blue skies, white fluffy clouds and hot air balloons. I tore the comic out of the paper and shoved into my pocket just as my meal arrived. Don't remember what happened the rest of the night but I trust that you too will see that, moment-by-moment, if we let it, life offers us everything we need to flourish in abundance. But there is one catch: we have to be willing and ready to see it.

CHAPTER 28
— A Dream —

*H*ad a dream that I called Stephanie's cell phone, even though I knew she wouldn't answer, but to my surprise she did answer! I knew it was a miracle when I heard her voice on the other end, "Hello Jonas."

"Stephanie!" I yelled amazed and happy beyond belief, "Please, tell me something, tell me anything!"

"I want you to stop calling me."

"But why?" I asked.

"Because I don't want to talk to you."

"But why don't you want to talk to me?" I asked confused, and little hurt.

"Well, it's not that I don't want to talk to you, it's just that I can't; I'm dead."

"Then how are we going to communicate with each other?" I asked.

"Just listen to your heart."

CHAPTER 29
— I See Elephants —
February 3, 2008

I started seeing elephants. Whenever I closed my eyes the image of an elephant would come to me as a vision. I would go to a restaurant and there would be an elephant on the wall as a decoration. I would go to a friend's house and there would be a flower pot shaped like and elephant. A woman would have a necklace with an elephant charm. *"What does this mean?"* I asked. *"Elephants never forget,"* came the answer. *"What am I not supposed to forget?"* The song from the children's television show *Sharon, Lois and Bram's Baby Elephant Show* came to me. *"Skinnamarinky dinky dink, skinnamarinky doo: I love you."* That's what the elephant visions were trying to tell me. *"Never forget that I love you."* That was a nice message but then the image of John McCain came to me and confused me even more. The elephants kept coming so I continued to question. One day in January 2008 I was at *Ocean State Job* Lot in Palmer and I saw a whole shelf filled with stuffed animal elephants. Wanting to understand what these elephants really meant I investigated closely. I pick up one of the elephants. On its belly were these words, *"Dream Big."* I wondered,

"What am I supposed to dream of?" The way I saw it, a big dream is the type of dream that if you told anyone about it they would laugh at you and say, *"There is no way you can do that!"* So that's what I set out to do. What could I dream up that others would think impossible?

The New England Patriots were going to the Super Bowl that year. Wouldn't it be awesome to perform my magic at their private Super Bowl party right after the game? Yes it would! I told others about it and they thought I was crazy. I knew I was onto something. I sent out a few emails asking for a favor from a friend and sure enough I got myself invited to perform at the Patriots Super Bowl Party in Scottsdale Arizona at the *Westin Kierland Hotel*! It wasn't a paid gig; in fact I lost money on the travel expenses. But I dreamt big, just like the elephant asked, and I achieved it. And what a cool gig it was! On February 3, 2008 I was the opening act for Earth Wind and Fire and Alicia Keys in the grand ballroom! I performed my sponge ball routine for Patriot Richard Seymour, and did my Ambitious Card routine for Patriot Larry Izzo! I got my business card in the hands of some very high profile people who put on high profile parties right in my area. Yeah, that was a cool gig.

There is a danger in dreaming small, and that danger is that we will achieve it. The only danger in dreaming big is that we might not get it, but we certainly will have a lot of fun going after it and we will have achieved so much more than we would have if we instead stifled our dreams.

On a side note, I had very little money for the Arizona trip; I actually had to borrow the money from a good friend to pay for the flight. Plus I couldn't afford a hotel. What is a guy to do? I did the logical thing and made friends with people at the party. Before the party even began I started chatting up the head of security, a man Paul. Turns out we had a bit in common; he's a bit of an amateur magician himself and is originally from Cambridge, MA.

As the evening went on I hinted that I didn't have a place to stay that night. "You can stay at my place! I have plenty of room!" What a huge act of trust for both of us. I barely knew this guy and he barely knew me, and yet he opened up his home. We pulled an all nighter at the party so we were both exhausted on the way to his place. That was when he started cracking serial killer jokes which, considering the circumstances, I thought was rather inappropriate. But I was too tired to care.

I slept most of the next day resting from the day before. Paul offered to drive me to the airport so that I didn't have to get a cab. On the way there he continued with the serial killer jokes before finally saying, "I probably shouldn't be making these jokes should I?"

I said, "They way I see it, if you were planning on killing me you would have done it by now."

There was a long delay at the airport because of the weather and I missed all of my connecting flights so I had to rearrange my whole itinerary. It was now the middle of the night and my flight wasn't until 7AM the next morning. There was no one left in the terminal save for those stranded from the same flight and the cleaning staff. I laid down on a bench and took my cell phone out. I looked at the two text messages that Stephanie had sent me just one week before she passed. *"I love you!"* and *"You're my everything!"* I loved looking at those messages. I'd read them several times a day. I set the alarm on the phone to go off so that I wouldn't miss the flight and placed it next to my head on the bench, literally right under my nose. I wanted to make sure that I heard it! I dosed off for a few minutes before waking up suddenly to the commotion of a cleaning woman nearby. I reached for my phone to look at the text messages again. But it wasn't there. My cell phone was gone! I asked the cleaning woman but she didn't know anything, so I went to security who in turn called the Phoenix Police Department. I filed a report with them and they said they would call me if the phone turned up. Stephanie's messages were gone.

Stephanie had arranged the whole thing. "I know I looked at them a lot Stephanie, but I liked them," I said to her out loud. I was holding myself back by holding onto them. Stephanie had to let them go for me and if I didn't start letting go of my other attachments more would be ripped from my hands too. My job was to accept that they were gone just as I had to accept her passing. We don't realize why we do something until we do it, for everything happens for a greater meaning.

CHAPTER 30
— Valentine's Day —
February 14, 2008

*T*urned into the cemetery. Stephanie had talked about this day six months earlier but I don't think this is what she had in mind. Or was it? The ground was iced over with frozen snow which during the first snow fall of the season really bothered me and ended in me getting kicked out of the cemetery. By now the grounds men were used to me.

The plan was to uncover her grave but the snow was so frozen that it was impossible. I would instead simply write a love note in the snow and place a single white rose above her grave. I would play my saxophone for her, the song that years earlier had cast the magic spell to materialize Stephanie in front of me when I opened my eyes. Seeing Stephanie that day was not to be, but experiencing her was.

I slowly pulled my car around the winding lanes as I listened to the car radio. I forget what was playing however I do remember what song came on just as I pulled beside Stephanie's grave and put the car into park. I should not have been surprised; months earlier Stephanie had asked for something special on Valentine's Day but instead it was she that did something special for me. The song that came on the radio just as I put the car into park was our song, *Live Like You Were Dying*. I looked at the passenger seat where just months earlier Stephanie had sat during our journey ride to the lake when our song had first magically appeared through the static. Now through the static of the spirit world was Stephanie giving me her Valentine's Day present. I smiled. I sang. I cried uncontrollably. It was the best Valentine's Day ever.

CHAPTER 31
— So Below —
April 2, 2008

I sat in my apartment, thinking. Thinking about my life's time. Of all the things I've done and how it's been. And I couldn't help but believe that I just didn't care anymore. I didn't want to live anymore yet I also didn't want to die anymore. I just didn't want to exist anymore.

Then suddenly, from outside in the distance came the sound of inspiration: I heard the train coming, riding down the bend. I jumped up and ran to the door, threw it open and ran towards the nearest crossing to catch the train to take my blues away. Never ran so fast in all of my life yet now to end it all I hurried as fast as I could. The wind in my face felt new, as if I had never felt it before; and I thought to myself, *"I'm going to miss being alive."*

The red warning lights were already flashing at the crossing when I turned the corner and the train's whistle grew louder as the approaching white light loomed nearer. But something else was there that didn't belong. A dark figure stood in the path of the oncoming train! My steps grew faster and just when I was upon the crossing the figure turned towards me and I saw the eyes of a familiar desperate man. I dove into him, pushing him off track, just as the train went crashing by. I wrestled with the man below me before I discovered that there was no one below. It was just me.

CHAPTER 32
— A Miracle —
August 1, 2008

I was having another one of those days. It wasn't my night to work but I ended up at *Samuel's Sports Bar* anyway. It was a Friday and I just needed a drink. The anniversary was coming up and I wasn't handling it very well; that and earlier that day my sunglasses snapped in half. They could no longer serve the purpose that they were made for and I had to let them go. *"Perhaps Stephanie also no longer served the purpose she was meant for in life and that's we she left and so I must let her go too?"* I didn't like that thought.

I was drunker than drunk in no time gulping down five appletinis in the course of time that would take the average person to drink a single beer. Stephanie had introduced me to the drink just weeks before she passed; she told me that it was one of her favorite drinks. After she passed I started drinking them for her because she couldn't anymore, even though until then I had never had so much as a drop of liquor in my life. I had become an alcoholic overnight.

After the fifth appletini I stumbled outside and collapsed on the sidewalk crying hysterically.

It was not a pretty sight. It was then that a man appeared from around the corner.

"Hey man," he asked, "are you all right?"

"Yeah, I'm going to be all right," I said, "How about you, what's your story?" Turns out the man was in trouble and needed some help.

"I'm not doing too good man. I'm out of gas, out of money, and I have to get my pregnant wife back home to Hartford."

"I can help you out my friend." I took out my wallet and handed him all of the money I had, which wasn't much as I spent most of it on appletinis.

Seeing my wallet now empty the man asked, "Are you sure? Are you going to be all right without this?"

"Oh yes," I said, "I'll be all right. Think about this, what do you see when you see a goose?"

"I don't know; what?"

"Never mind," I was too drunk to get into it, "I only wish I could give you more." Inspiration struck. "In fact, I have one more thing for you." I reached into my pocket and pulled out my business card wallet. From it I pulled out my one last dollar bill from behind Stephanie's picture. "I'm a magician. I perform miracles." I folded the dollar bill into eighths. "Whatever we want in this life, no matter what it is, we can have it," then I unfolded the bill, "that's why when we dream we have to dream big." In that moment the one dollar bill transformed into a one hundred dollar bill! "This is for you," I said handing it to the man.

Whenever I perform magic I go out there with the intention of performing miracles. I don't want participants to ask, *"How did that happen?"* or *"Why did that happen"* but rather to ask *"How does that make me feel?"* I want to touch their emotions and make them question their feelings, not their intellect. That is just what I did that drunken night outside the bar collapsed on the sidewalk. That man answered that important question. He answered by hugging me and crying.

"Thank you man, thank you so much! This means so much to me! Thank you!" Then he left.

Miracles do happen. Prayers are answered. We just have to be open to experiencing them. And in this case perhaps drunk too. No longer crying, the experience put a smile on my face. What we do to one we also do to ourselves; which is why we have to be careful what we do to others. For we are all One.

On a side note, my alcohol hobby had dipped into my funds and I was now out of money. That hundred dollar bill I gave the man was actually a very special hundred dollar bill. It was the original hundred that I used back in August 2007 when I first started performing that trick after creating it, inspired by Stephanie. On August 17,

2007 while visiting Stephanie at her apartment I performed the piece for her.

She grabbed the bill from my hand and said, "How did you do that!?!"

"I'll show you," I said. That's a bold statement for a magician to make for magicians are not supposed to reveal their secrets.

"You can't tell me!" She said, "You're a magician, you're not supposed to."

"But I don't want keep any secrets from you."

"No, don't. I don't want to know."

When Stephanie passed away I framed that hundred dollar bill and hung it on my wall with the inscription below it, "You inspire me..." But with money running out I had to take that very special bill off the wall in order to perform the piece. She was my hundred dollar bill. And so when I handed the man the hundred dollar bill I was giving him more than a hundred dollars. I was giving him a memory, an artifact from the most important, most wonderful time of my life. And yet I was ok with it. That hundred dollar bill was meant to inspire others to dream big and to make those dreams come true. Even if it's as simple of a dream as getting your family home safely. Surely that is a dream worth coming true and surely that hundred dollar bill is doing far more good now that it is set free than it was as a prisoner on my wall. Slowly, I am starting letting go.

CHAPTER 33
— I Just Happened The Other Day —
November 1, 2008

Stephanie would so often begin telling a story by saying, *"It just happened the other day,"* even if what she was talking about happened years earlier. Likewise I would begin a story by saying, *"It's a true story,"* even if I'm making it up. We had shared countless adventures together over the years and one day we decided we would write a book together telling those stories. We already had a title for it: *It Just Happened the Other Day: A True Story.* But we never got the chance write the book while she was alive.

In the time since Stephanie's passing my magic changed. I began seeing it as a metaphor for life and so in my search for answers and to deal with my grief my performances started to transform, mirroring the transformation that I too was going through. Stereotypically magic is seen as a bunch of illusions with people shoved into boxes. Whether it's putting someone inside to be sawn in half or to make someone disappear magicians are oft to use boxes as a means to demonstrate their abilities. But why is that? In contemporary culture it is cliché to say "think outside the box" but that is exactly what the magician is saying. What does this mean? This "box" we are given is reality, a reality passed down from generation to generation. To "think outside the box" is to actually leave the illusion of reality that this box has given us. It is just like the fish in an aquarium. To the fish the aquarium is all that they know; even though it is a false reality, it is all that there is to their world. Yet as human beings we know that there is a whole ocean that the fish could be swimming in. Surely if there is a whole other world for the fish there must surely also be a whole other world for us. The dilemma is that even if the fish become aware of the ocean, if they were to jump out of their "box" they would simply fall to the floor and die. It is therefore the job of the magician to bring humanity's proverbial "aquarium" to the ocean so that we can swim free with the fishes in the sea. With these ideas my performances started taking on a deeper meaning as I found deeper meaning in life. That's when a new type of magic show started to take form in July of 2008.

Everything moved so quickly. Even before I was finished with the script I booked the theatre, *City Stage* in downtown Springfield. Before we went into dress rehearsals we started selling tickets. Everything just happened so quickly. The production had turned into much more than I had imagined, now more of a magical play than just a magic show, combining magic with music and poetry to tell the story. When we finally made it to the full dress rehearsals in October of 2008, just weeks before the premier, I recalled a conversation that I had with Stephanie back in March of 2006.

"Wouldn't it be fun to do a play?" Stephanie asked. I was in Winter Park Florida visiting my good friend Matt. It had only been a month since Stephanie and I had reconnected and she called almost every day to talk with me.

"That does sound like a lot fun Stephanie," I said "there are a lot of local community theatres in the area, let's join one."

"Don't say you will if you don't plan on doing it," she said sternly. I was taken aback by her sudden lack of confidence in me. What had I done for her to not believe my word?

"I wouldn't say I would do it if I didn't mean it," I said. "I promise you Stephanie, we will do a play together."

We never did that play. But it did occur to me (just the other day) that the play Stephanie was talking about is this play, and that is why Stephanie put so much importance on making me promise to keep my word. This production is our life's work; our sacred contract. The play asks people to dream big regardless of circumstance and motivates them to act on those dreams. A world so blessed will be a peaceful world indeed. The title of the production honors the book we never got to write, *It Just Happened the Other Day: A True Story*. By sharing our story I am fulfilling my promise to Stephanie and through the performance it will be a shining Light for others to be guided.

In the weeks leading up to premier I asked Stephanie for guidance. A clear yet unique sign that she was helping me and happy with my plans. Specifically, I asked that she show me pennies. People often down play such signs, saying that one only finds meaning in something when the individual assigns a meaning to it; but for me, as soon as I asked Stephanie for this sign and I started seeing pennies everywhere and it validated what I already felt in my heart. Everywhere I went I found pennies: on the side walk, at the movie theatre, at rehearsals. Then just three days before the premier of our show Stephanie led me to a pile of pennies...a whole *pile* of pennies! The afternoon of the premier I showed up to the theatre early and walked into my dressing room. I looked down and there it was. Right in the middle of the dressing room was a shinny 2007 penny. "Thank you Stephanie," I said out loud, "we're going to have a great night."

And that we did. Stephanie showed up on stage, performing alongside me and the crew. On a side table on stage left during *The Blue Door* sequence there was a picture frame with a photograph of Stephanie. Right in the middle of the sequence just before my assistant Amanda (playing the part of Stephanie) was about to appear in the doorway, Stephanie made her presence known. She pushed over her picture frame. The entire theatre jumped! There was no doubt about it; there was no way it could have fallen on its own, it was pushed over. "She's here!" I said, and then opened the door and there was Amanda smiling.

Nearing the end of the show I was restrained in a straitjacket and Amanda was performing a piece of magic for me. She was performing the signed silk napkin to inside a bell pepper effect by contemporary Canadian magician Carl Cloutier. Being opening night I was excited to see how Amanda would do considering she had never done a magic trick before in her life. She did great, with Stephanie's help. In case the pennies and knocking over of the photograph wasn't enough Stephanie wanted to make sure that I knew that she truly was going to be at all of my magic shows from now on. When Amanda stepped into the audience to have a woman draw a picture on the red silk napkin the woman drew a butterfly. "Of course you did," I said.

Life really is a lot like a puzzle. Crazy experiences will often be presented to us and we will want to fight them, wondering how such terrible things could possibly fit into our life. But then one day, if we keep going and never give up and never give in to temptations that threaten to stop us, the pieces begin to fall into place, revealing a beautiful picture. It may not be the picture that we had expected but it will be the picture that we were born to be. A picture that is us.

CHAPTER 34
— A True Story —
November 20, 2008

I had just pulled onto 91 South in Holyoke, MA when I looked in the rearview mirror. I had just finished the second performance of *It Just Happened the Other Day: A True Story*. Driving behind me was Jeff Pyzocha, my good friend and prop manager. He had the Blue Door in the back of his pickup truck and I was checking to be sure he was still behind me as we would be storing the door at his place for night. Jeff didn't know how to get to the highway from the theatre so I lead us to 91 and he was to pass me so I could follow him back to his place. That was the plan anyway.

It was dark but I could clearly see the silhouette of the solid two-hundred pound door against the headlights of a tractor trailer truck. I was about to look away when the Blue Door flew out of the back of Jeff's truck and into the air like a bird taking flight. It was beautiful! Then it slammed into the front of the tractor trailer truck shattering into pieces of nothing.

"No," I said out loud, "that didn't just happen." Then Jeff began flashing his lights and pulled to the side of the highway. "Damn it! It did happen!" I pulled Old Bertha to the side of the highway as Jeff pulled up behind me and the tractor trailer truck slowed down and parked in front of us. Called 911 and told the operator, "A tractor trailer truck just went through a big blue door on 91 South in Holyoke." It took some explaining but I convinced her that it wasn't a prank.

Got out of the car and looked back to see where the door was, but there was nothing left. That's when Jeff got out of his pickup and apologized profusely. I said to him, "Years from now we're going to look back at this night and just laugh and laugh, so why don't' we just laugh now?" He didn't see my logic. I explained further, "This is my show, not yours. Any damage caused by it is my fault alone. I am the one to be held responsible; not you or anyone else. Before we left the theatre I should have checked that the door was properly secured, but I didn't. This is my fault; no one else's." He felt a little better.

When the trooper showed up we took care of the paperwork. The truck driver was surprisingly calm. They are a rare breed after all; hitting a giant blue door on the highway is just another day for them. The damage to the tractor trailer truck was minimal, but all I could think about was what would have happened if a car was behind Jeff's truck instead of a big tractor trailer truck. Someone surely would have died. It occurred to me then that I was supposed to be right behind the Jeff's truck, following him to his house. It was supposed to have killed me. *"Thank You God for Jeff's bad sense of direction."*

The accident gave me a nervous twitch in my eye giving me the nickname "Blinky" from some of my friends. Took some time off from the show to reflect on all that had happened. The blue door incident was not the first of unfortunate events. In the weeks leading up to the premier my roommate and I were evicted from our apartment. I had put nearly every cent of my income into this production and had fallen behind on the rent as a result. Landlords don't take kindly to that. During that same time my car broke down making it difficult to move out of the apartment. Somehow I found a new apartment, moved out of my old place and into the new place, all while continuing dress rehearsals for the show and all during the week of the premier.

Despite these obstacles, opening night went on without a hitch, and even with the Blue Door destroyed we rebuilt it for performances three and four the following year. After reflecting on the negative occurrences I weighed them in respect to the responses I received from those who experienced the show. Their stories of healing, hope and transformation confirmed for me that what I was doing mattered, and no matter what obstacles I faced I would not let anything get in my way of helping others and would endure till the end. All my life I had pursued the ultimate in magic; the wonders of my imagination where anything and everything is possible. Now I see that it is not found in simply performing magic tricks, rather it is in sharing Peace, Love and Joy.

CHAPTER 35
— Keeping Promises —

I had promised Stephanie I would attend church with her family on Sunday, but when she asked me it was a Sunday night so that Sunday was out. The following Sunday we were at the lake so that Sunday was out. We agreed that the following Sunday we would go, but then she ran out of Sundays. I wasn't sure if she meant for me to attend just that one time or if she wanted me to go often, so I began going to church every week just in case. I was sitting in the pew one morning after a night of heavy drinking and my mind wondered again to thoughts of self-destruction. The Priest's words spoke to me:

> *"To be physically blind and unable to experience the beauty of a sunset is sad, and yet to be spiritually blind and unable to experience the beauty of a life itself is a true tragedy."*

These words spoke to my broken heart and extinguished spirit. Death — a beautiful sunset of a life well lived. I thought of the setting sun just months earlier on the go-carts. I thought of how happy Stephanie was, even though she had run out of Sundays. Everything truly was perfect. I smiled, even through the tears.

CHAPTER 36
— A Dream —

*H*ad a dream that I was at Stephanie's wake and I knelt down at her casket to pray. And when I did she awoke and looked into my eyes.

Surprised by this I at first didn't know what to say. All I got out was, "Stephanie, please tell me something; anything at all."

"You mean something that I'd like you to know?" she asked

"Yes," I replied.

Her face lit up with the brightest smile I had ever seen as she said, "You love me so much! With all of your heart and soul! You are all about me!"

"Yes Stephanie. I do. I am," I said.

"But you have the potential to be all about you."

Then I woke up.

For now is the time to awaken and let go. And now is the time to listen to my heart and to live.

CHAPTER 37
— Bicycle Ride —

Three frogs sat on a log.
One frog decided it was time to jump off the log
and swim in the water.

How many frogs remain on the log?

One would think that there are now only two,
yet in truth there remain three:
for the frog that wanted to swim
only <u>decided</u> to jump off the log,
yet never acted on its decisions.

----

*T*here is a moment when the caterpillar is no longer a caterpillar yet is not quite a butterfly. It has entered its chrysalis where it will grow wings to explore life transformed. So it is also for humankind. During this time of transformation we must leave all that we've ever known for a new reality; a world beyond the inherited veil of illusionary reality given to us by those who have come before. We must not view this merely as an end but rather as a means to an end; the beginning of something more. After all, is it not so that every new beginning comes from some other beginning's end?

I have decided to jump off my log and swim in the water. I have taken away my resources to be content, for no comfortable individual will ever do anything to improve his or herself. This truth is reflected in the words of Steve Jobs from his speech to Stanford University graduates in 2005, *"Stay hungry; stay foolish."* I am hungry. I am foolish. Literally. There is no choice now but to act on my decisions. Any other way would contradict my morals and prostitute my values.

We never truly know why we imagine such things until the day that a few key pieces of the puzzle fill in the space between dream and reality, revealing a beautiful picture; a picture that's always been there but hidden behind the mystery of study, preparation, experience and reflection.

I have a dream of going on a bicycle ride. Not merely a ride around town nor a day trip, but a journey! Lasting days, weeks, months, years! Perhaps the bicycle ride is my ticket to freedom; a freedom to go where I was born to go, and to be who I was born to be.

CHAPTER 38
— Journey of Discovery —
April 2, 2008

I stood on the railroad tracks of a dark lonely road waiting for the train to take my blues away. It was waiting there that a tree spoke to me. Considering the circumstances I listened closely to what the tree had to say; after all, a tree had never before spoken to me. At least not that I had ever noticed.

"You are on a journey of discovery," said the tree.

"What am I supposed to discover?" I asked, "And where am I to journey to?"

But the tree never answered. Without any words I knew that any answer to my questions would only make more questions. In that moment I also understood that I had discovered that journey I had been looking for all my life. Recognizing that, I pushed myself off the dark track and took the path of Light. My fate is up to me and no one else. There is no one above me and there is no one below me. It is just me. And what a beautiful picture it is!

BOOKS BY JONAS CAIN

It Just Happened The Other Day:
A True Story

One day two best friends decided to write a book together. Before a word was even written they already had a title for it. Whenever Stephanie told a story she would begin by saying, "It just happened the other day," even if it had actually happened months earlier; and whenever Jonas told a story he would begin by saying, "It's a true story," even when what he was saying was actually a joke. Due to unforeseen circumstances, the pair never got to write their book...until now.

A poignant true story of love, loss, and inspired hope, It Just Happened the Other Day: A True Story is sure to touch the heart of all readers.

Just Another Day

The long awaited sequel to It Just Happened the Other Day: A True Story, this book opens on just another day for Jonas Cain as he embarks on a cross-country bicycle ride, from MA to L.A. Detailing his ensuing detours, this book highlights that the actual destination truly matters little when you're on an adventure.

Journey Of Discovery:
Awaken Your Inner Power

A book you can read in an hour or keep on your nightstand for daily inspiration, Journey of Discovery: Awaken Your Inner Power offers concise practical ideas for bringing your inner purpose to Light. If approached with an open heart and an honest mind, this material is sure to help you on your journey to awaken your inner power.

And The Pursuit Of Happiness

What does it mean to be happy? Is it a physical sensation of pleasure, or if it more of an attitude? Is it resiliency won by virtuous living, or is it satisfaction with the state of affairs? Can we be happy even if don't feel happy?

This book examines these questions by exploring various theories of happiness from philosophical and practical perspectives, while also exploring the author's own earnest attempts at applying these theories. *...and the Pursuit of Happiness* is a concise guide meant to help you rediscover Happiness again for the first time. Are YOU ready to be happy?

The Problem Of Poverty

By examining the individual and structural causes of poverty, and the political, religious, and ethical perspectives of society's obligation to the poor, this preliminary study aims to suggest an innovative course of action to deal with this social problem. This proposed prescription will have a focused emphasis on individual responsibility implemented in pockets of localized communities that when duplicated across regions will demonstrate significant national success.

Absurd Jokes

Inspired by the time Jonas figured out the meaning of the term Pittsburgh Steelers, after being mugged on the streets of Pittsburgh, this book suggests a mathematical equation for humor:

$$tragedy + time = humor$$

This edited compilation of Jonas Cain's all-time favorite jokes aims to offer readers inspiration to find solace in the humor of life's tragedies.

Magic Words

Leveraging his over twenty-year career as a magician, *Magic Words* is Jonas Cain's tome of over 52 Magic Words presented and explained to help readers quickly and easily implement these words into their daily lives to conjure personal and professional growth. Read it straight through cover-to-cover, or keep it on your nightstand for daily encouragement, either way *Magic Words* will engage and empower you to Boldly Step Forward PERFORM!

Are You P.O.S.I.T.I.V.E.?

Positivity is often misunderstood to mean putting on a pair of rose-colored glasses, pretending that everything is fine and dandy, even when everything isn't fine and dandy. But Jonas Cain holds that this understanding of positivity is flawed, arguing that true positivity can not ignore reality but instead has to reflect an honest assessment of the truth.

Are Your P.O.S.I.T.I.V.E.? will take you on an 8-step journey that will encourage you to "rethink positive thinking," opening you to a life of engagement and empowerment!

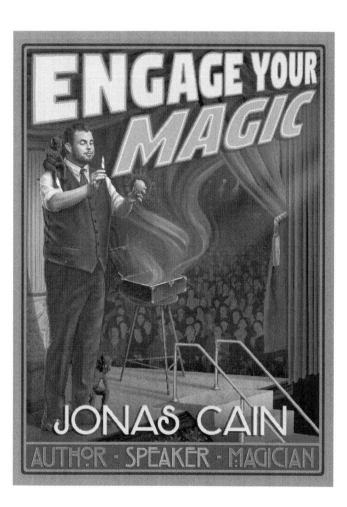

TESTIMONIALS

Positivity Runs In His Blood!

"His delivery is such a creative and fun way to get such strong and important messages through. The world needs more Jonas Cain's in it. Positivity runs in his blood! We are managers of assisted living and memory care communities. We need positivity and laughter to be able to provide the highest quality of care to our residents. Jonas made us laugh, think and be in the moment."

Angela Pelletier / Director of Operations
WoodBine Senior Living / Marriottsville, MD
★★★★★

Leaves You Feeling Stronger!

"Jonas is a special talent. His capacity for magic goes beyond mere entertainment as it delves into the educational, the emotional, and the spiritual. He will leave you feeling stronger. A true professional."

Daniel Lavoie / Vice President
BayBoston Capital / Boston, MA
★★★★★

More Than I Expected!

"Jonas did a great job with a real tough crowd. More than I expected!"

John Roberson / General Manager
Marr Crane & Rigging / Boston, MA
★★★★★

Hope To Do Business With You Again!

"Thank you so much for your preparation, presentation, message and information that you gave us. The motivation and magic are a great pairing. I hope to do business with you again in the future!"

Matt Lambert / General Manager
Empire Beauty School / Rochester, NH

★★★★★

This Will Become An Annual Staple For My Teams!

"Jonas spoke to my boys and girls track teams the day before our league championship meet, and took the time to personalize and tailor a program to our specific needs about setting goals and finding a personal path toward success. Both teams won! This will be an annual staple for my teams!"

James Fletcher / Coach
Woburn High School Track Team / Woburn, MA

★★★★★

Will Absolutely Recommend Him To Anybody!

"The most engaging, fabulous, fantastic speech...loved it! The staff was engaged, and he was fantastic, cool, calm, and collected. We love Jonas and will absolutely recommend him to anybody and will bring him back!"

Kristie Balisciano / Marketing Manager
Easterseals / Greater Waterbury, CT

★★★★★

Lively & Engaging!

"The presentations were lively and engaging! So many of our students do not have access to communication at home and as a result, it is on us as a school to provide character education. This was an absolutely perfect way to do it! The students now understand that there are more people out there who care about molding them into good citizens. It is often difficult to find people who understand how to work with deaf people and use interpreters, are willing to work directly with the students, and understand their challenges. I truly appreciate Jonas' willingness to work with a variety of people as well as taking the time beforehand (and afterwards!) to really understand his audience."

Erika Kaftan / Assistant Director of Education Services
Willie Ross School for the Deaf / Longmeadow, MA

Lessons That Will Last A Lifetime!

"Jonas' message of kindness and positivity was sprinkled throughout effortlessly. The connections he made with magic and having good character are lessons that will last a lifetime. Both adults and students were amazed by Jonas' talent. Most importantly, Jonas loves what he does and that shines through from beginning to end!"

Molly Cole / School Psychologist
Hatfield Elementary School / Hatfield, MA

Highest Level Of Professionalism

"Jonas demonstrated the highest level of professionalism ... he was enthusiastic and clear in his instruction and managed to engage those normally resistant students in the learning he was presenting."

Mindy Rosengarten / Teacher
Ware Junior & Senior High School / Ware, MA
★★★★★

More Than Magic...It's A Life Lesson!

"The beauty of his magic is that it is more than just that; it's a life lesson. I walked away from one of these shows both happy I got to see the magic, but also uplifted. A great person, a great showman, and a great life lesson taught that can apply to all."

Jeffrey Feely / Project Manager
Fuze / Boston, MA
★★★★★

Makes You Think In A Deeply Introspective Way!

"I could not recommend him highly enough. He makes you think in a deeply introspective way. One of Jonas's great talents is that not only does he greatly entertain ... but he also shares a story and makes you think long after the show is over."

Michael Carley / Technical Solutions Engineer
Oracle / Reston, VA
★★★★★

Such A Huge Heart!

"Jonas is a one in a million type guy. He has a huge heart and is willing to help anyone out that needs it. I have met many mentors through the Boys State program, but Jonas stands out among them all because of his dedication to helping others succeed and helping them achieve their goals."

Chris MacRae / Assurance Senior
EY / Boston, MA
★★★★★

Funny & Entertaining!

"The students truly enjoyed Jonas Cain's presentation. He was funny and entertaining. Most importantly, he communicated an amazing and positive message using his Magic tricks in which all the students could relate to and make their own!"

Sister Kathleen Marie / Principal
St. Denis-St. Columba School / Hopewell Junction, NY
★★★★★

You Help People See the Light in the Dark!

"Your true talent is inspiring people and uplifting their spirits. It is people like you that really help people to see the light through the dark. Thank you for being a true inspiration to us all!"

John F. / Springfield, MA
★★★★★

Makes You Fall In Love With Life!

"There is something at once innocent yet expert about him. He makes you fall in love with life. He is personable and beautiful. My cynical friend who I dragged to the show was even touched. And she's from Detroit!!"

Lisa Carver / Author of *25 Lives*

★★★★★

Warm, Friendly, Professional & Funny!

"Jonas exceeded our expectations. Everything went off without a hitch. We explained the tact we wanted to take with the entertainment and Jonas executed perfectly. We got so many nice compliments on Jonas's work. We'd definitely have him back. Warm, friendly, professional and funny and so talented. Thanks again Jonas!!!"

Carl D. / GigMasters.com Reviewer
Bloomfield, CT

★★★★★

Beyond Our Expectations!

"Jonas was early, extremely friendly, professional and the highlight of our event! He kept everyone entertained, and went above and beyond our expectations!"

Paul Gileno / Founder & President
U.S. Pain Foundation / Middletown, CT

★★★★★

Left Me With A Different Perspective On Life!

"Jonas' show was one that nearly moved me to tears. It was an emotional rollercoaster that left me with a different perspective on life and how to live it. Before the show, I had nearly given up on many of the life goals I had had since I was a child. After that night however, I was shown that you can achieve just about anything if you stick to it. Jonas is a man I will not soon forget. He and his story is one I shared with just about everyone I know."

Corbin Armstrong / Student
UMASS / Amherst, MA

Totally Entertained By His Quick Wit!

"Jonas performed before approximately 400 people on our stage for the USO anniversary variety show. He had everyone not only amazed by his magic but also totally entertained by his quick wit and humor! He is someone who is very sociable and likable. He is certainly someone who comes to mind immediately for our next event. I am happy we found him and would absolutely recommend him to everyone!"

Linda Disanti / Chicopee, MA

Huge Hit!

"Jonas came to our event to entertain the crowd (500-plus people). He was huge hit with both the kids and the adults! He brought his own set-up and didn't require any supervision at all, which was a relief because we were very busy with all the other aspects of the event. Several people told me how much they liked him and hoped he would be back again next year! Jonas was very professional, entertaining, and easy to work with, and I would highly recommend him to others!"

Trisha Blanchet / Founder & President
Operation Delta Dog / Massachusetts

Absolutely Amazing!

"Jonas was absolutely amazing! Our crowd can bit a bit sarcastic and hard to handle. Jonas was great on the spot and his tricks were great. Super funny and accommodating! All my friends were impressed and said it was such a good time. He made my husband's 50th birthday party a blast. Thanks again!"

Maria Riopel / Manager
Laskara Restaurant / Wallingford, CT

ABOUT THE AUTHOR

Read the book.

CONNECT WITH JONAS!